M000076539

JOURNEYING TOWARDS THE SPIRITUAL

A Digest of *The Spiritual Man*

by Watchman Nee

in 42 Lessons

Christian Fellowship Publishers, Inc.
New York

JOURNEYING TOWARDS THE SPIRITUAL

A Digest of *The Spiritual Man*
by Watchman Nee
in 42 Lessons

Copyright © 2006
Christian Fellowship Publishers, Inc.
New York
All Right Reserved

ISBN 13: 978-0-935008-86-9
ISBN 10: 0-935008-86-1

Available from the Publishers at:

11515 Allecingie Parkway
Richmond, Virginia 23235

www.c-f-p.com

Printed in the United States of America

Foreword

God's desire is to commune with man. God being spirit, the man who worships Him must worship in spirit and truth. It is therefore essential for man to be spiritual. This is what the gospel of Jesus Christ is all about. Salvation is the way to spirituality.

The three volume set of *The Spiritual Man* by Watchman Nee serves as a guide, not as a manual, to walk in spiritual life as well as to fight the spiritual warfare. It was written under tremendous spiritual conflict. Only through the grace of God and the victory of Christ was Watchman Nee able to finish the writing. Now having become a Christian classic, it may be considered Watchman Nee's legacy to the Church.

However, this being such a large book of 694 pages, a digest of it seems to be urgently needed. There are altogether 42 chapters dealing with the 42 different aspects of *The Spiritual Man*. This reminds us of the 42 stations of the journey of the children of Israel from Rameses in Egypt to the plains of Moab by the river Jordan opposite Jericho (see Numbers 33). Hence, there are 42 lessons to be learned in journeying towards the spiritual. May we be guided by the Spirit of God to heartily learn these necessary lessons all to the glory of God.

CONTENTS

Contents

LESSON ONE

SPIRIT, SOUL, AND BODY

May the God of peace himself sanctify you wholly, and may your spirit and soul and body be kept sound and blameless at the coming of our Lord Jesus Christ.

1 Thessalonians 5.23

The ordinary concept of the constitution of human beings is dualistic—soul and body. According to this concept soul is the invisible inner spiritual part, while body is the visible outer corporal part. Though there is some truth to this, it is nevertheless inaccurate. Such an opinion comes from fallen man, not from God; apart from God's revelation, no concept is dependable. That the body is man's outward sheath is undoubtedly correct, but the Bible never confuses spirit and soul as though they are the same. Not only are they different in terms; their very natures differ from each other. The Word of God does not divide man into the two parts of soul and body. It treats man, rather, as tripartite—spirit, soul, and body. First Thessalonians 5.23 reads: "May the God of peace himself sanctify you wholly; and may your spirit and soul and body be kept sound and blameless at the coming of our Lord Jesus Christ." This verse precisely shows that the whole man is divided into three parts. The Apostle Paul refers here to the complete sanctification of believers, "sanctify you *wholly*." According to the Apostle, how is a person wholly sanctified? By his spirit and soul and body being kept. From this we can easily understand that the *whole* person comprises these three parts. This verse also makes a distinction between spirit and soul; otherwise, Paul would have said simply "your soul." Since God has distinguished the human spirit from the human soul, we conclude that man is composed of not two, but three, parts: spirit, soul, and body.

Is it a matter of any consequence to divide spirit and soul? It is an issue of *supreme* importance for it affects tremendously the spiritual life of a believer. How can a believer understand spiritual life if he does not know what is the extent of the realm of the spirit? Without such understanding how can he grow spiritually? To fail to distinguish between spirit and soul is fatal to spiritual maturity. Christians often account what is soulical as spiritual, and thus they remain in a soulish state and seek not what is really spiritual. How can we escape loss if we confuse what God has divided?

Other portions of the Scriptures make this same differentiation between spirit and soul. "For the word of God is living and active, sharper than any two-edged sword, piercing to the division of *soul and spirit*, of joints and marrow, and discerning the thoughts and intentions of the heart" (Hebrews 4.12). The writer in this verse divides man's non-corporal elements into two parts, "soul and spirit." The corporal part is mentioned here as including the joints and marrow—organs of motion and sensation. When the priest uses the sword to cut and completely dissect the sacrifice, nothing inside can be hidden. Even joint and marrow are separated. In like manner the Lord Jesus uses the Word of God on His people to separate thoroughly, to pierce even to the division of the spiritual, the soulical, and the physical. And from this it follows that since soul and spirit can be *divided*, they must be different in nature. It is thus evident here that man is a composite of three parts.

THE CREATION OF MAN

"And Jehovah God formed man of dust from the ground, and breathed into his nostrils the breath of life; and man became a living soul" (Genesis 2.7 ASV). When God first created man He formed him of dust from the ground, and then breathed "the breath of life" into his nostrils. As soon as the breath of life, which became man's spirit, came into contact with man's body, the soul was produced. Hence the soul is the combination of man's body and spirit. The Scriptures therefore call man "a living soul." The breath of life became man's spirit; that is, the principle of life within him. The Lord Jesus tells us "it is the spirit that gives life" (John 6.63). This breath of life comes from the Lord of Creation. However, we must not confuse *man's* spirit with God's Holy Spirit. The latter differs from our human spirit. Romans 8.16 demonstrates their difference by declaring that "it is the Spirit himself bearing witness *with* our spirit that we are children of God." The original of the word "life" in "breath of life" is *chay* and is in the *plural*. This may refer to the fact that the inbreathing of God produced a twofold life, soulical and spiritual. When the inbreathing of God entered man's body it became the spirit of man; but when the spirit reacted with the body the soul was produced. This explains the source of our spiritual and soulical lives. We must recognize, though, that this spirit is not God's *Own* life, for "the breath of the Almighty gives me life" (Job 33.4). It is not the entrance of the untreated life of God into man, neither is it that life of God which we receive at regeneration. What we receive at new birth is God's Own life as typified by the tree of life. But our human spirit, though permanently existing, is void of "eternal life."

RESPECTIVE FUNCTIONS OF SPIRIT, SOUL, AND BODY

It is through the corporal body that man comes into contact with the material world. Hence we may label the body as that part which gives us *world-consciousness*. The soul comprises the intellect which aids us in the present state of existence and the emotions which proceed from the senses. Since the soul belongs to man's own self and reveals his personality, it is termed the part of *self-consciousness*. The spirit is that part by which we commune with God and by which alone we are able to apprehend and worship Him. Because it tells us of our relationship with God, the spirit is called the element of *God-*

3

consciousness. God dwells in the spirit, self dwells in the soul, while senses dwell in the body.

Of these three elements the spirit is the noblest for it joins with God. The body is the lowest for it contacts with matter. The soul lying between them joins the two together and also takes their character to be its own. The soul makes it possible for the spirit and the body to communicate and to cooperate. The work of the soul is to keep these two in their proper order so that they may not lose their right relationship—namely, that the lowest, the body, may be subjected to the spirit, and that the highest, the spirit, may govern the body through the soul. Man's prime factor is definitely the soul. It looks to the spirit to give what the latter has received from the Holy Spirit in order that the soul, after it has been perfected, may transmit what it has obtained to the body; then the body too may share in the perfection of the Holy Spirit and so become a spiritual body.

Actually the soul is the pivot of the entire being, because man's volition belongs to it. It is only when the soul is willing to assume a humble position that the spirit can ever manage the whole man. If the soul rebels against taking such a position the spirit will be powerless to rule. This explains the meaning of the free will of man. Man is not an automaton that turns according to God's will. Rather, man has full sovereign power to decide for himself. He possesses the organ of his own volition and can choose either to follow God's will or to resist Him and follow Satan's will instead. God desires that the spirit, being the noblest part of man, should control the whole being. Yet, the will—the crucial part of individuality—belongs to the soul. It is the will which determines whether the spirit, the body, or even itself is to rule. In view of the fact that the soul possesses such power and is the organ of man's individuality, the Bible calls man "a living soul."

LESSON TWO

SPIRIT AND SOUL

My soul exalts the Lord, and my spirit has rejoiced in God my Savior.

Luke 1.46-47 (NASV)

SPIRIT

According to the teaching of the Bible and the experience of believers, the human spirit can be said to comprise three parts; or, to put it another way, one can say it has three main functions. These are conscience, intuition and communion. The *conscience* is the discerning organ which distinguishes right and wrong; not, however, through the influence of knowledge stored in the mind but rather by a spontaneous direct judgment. Often reasoning will justify things which our conscience judges. The work of the conscience is independent and direct; it does not bend to outside opinions. If man should do wrong it will raise its voice of accusation. *Intuition* is the sensing organ of the human spirit. It is so diametrically different from physical sense and soulical sense that it is called intuition. Intuition involves a direct sensing independent of any outside influence. That knowledge which comes to us without any help from the mind, emotion or volition comes intuitively. We really "know" through our intuition; our mind merely helps us to "understand." The revelations of God and all the movements of the Holy Spirit are known to the believer through his intuition. A believer must therefore heed these two elements: the voice of conscience and the teaching of intuition. *Communion* is worshiping God. The organs of the soul are incompetent to worship God. God is not apprehended by our thoughts, feelings or intentions, for He can only be known *directly* in our spirits. Our worship of God and God's communications with us are directly in the spirit. They take place in "the inner man," not in the soul or outward man.

We can conclude then that these three elements of conscience, intuition and communion are deeply interrelated and function coordinately. The relationship between conscience and intuition is that conscience judges according to intuition; it condemns all conduct which does not follow the directions given by intuition. Intuition is related to communion or worship in that God is known by man intuitively and reveals His will to man in the intuition. No measure of expectation or deduction gives us the knowledge of God.

Before the believer is born again his spirit becomes so sunken and surrounded by his soul that it is impossible for him to distinguish whether something is emanating from the soul or from the spirit. The functions of the latter have become mixed up with those of the former. Furthermore, the spirit has lost its primary function—towards God; for it is dead to God. It thus would appear that it has become an accessory to the soul. And as the mind, emotion and volition grow stronger, the functions of the spirit become so eclipsed as to render them almost unknown. That is why there must be the work of dividing between soul and spirit after a believer is regenerated.

SOUL

Aside from having a spirit which enables him to commune with God, man also possesses a soul, his self-consciousness. Hs is made conscious of his existence by the work of his soul. It is the seat of our personality. The elements which make us human belong to the soul. Intellect, thought, ideals, love, emotion, discernment, choice, decision, etc., are but various experiences of the soul.

It has been explained already that the spirit and the body are merged in the soul which, in turn, forms the organ of our personality. That is why the Bible sometimes calls man "soul," as though man has only this element. For example, Genesis 12.5 refers to people as "souls" (ASV). Again, when Jacob brought his entire family down to Egypt, it is recorded that "all the souls of the house of Jacob, that came into Egypt, were threescore and ten" (Genesis 46.27 ASV). Numerous instances occur in the original language of the Bible where "soul" is used instead of "man." For the seat and essence of the personality is the soul. To comprehend a man's personality is to comprehend his person. Man's existence, characteristics and life are all in the soul. The Bible consequently calls man "a soul."

That which constitutes man's personality are the three main faculties of volition, mind and emotion. Volition is the instrument for our decisions, revealing our power to choose. It expresses our willingness or unwillingness: "we will" or "we won't." Without it, man is reduced to an automaton. Mind, the instrument for our thoughts, manifests our intellectual power. Out of this arise wisdom, knowledge and reasoning. Lack of it makes a man foolish and dull. The instrument for our likes and dislikes is the faculty of emotion. Through it we are able to express love or hate and to feel joyful, angry, sad or happy. Any shortage of it will render man as insensitive as wood or stone.

THE SOUL LIFE

Some Bible scholars point out to us that three different words are employed in the Greek to designate "life": (1) *bios* (2) *psuche* (3) *zoe*. They all describe life but convey very different meanings. *Bios* has reference to the means of life or living. Our Lord Jesus used this word when He commended the woman who cast into the temple treasury her whole living. *Zoe* is the highest life, the life of the spirit. Whenever the Bible speaks of eternal life it uses this word. *Psuche* refers to the animated life of man, his natural life or the life of the soul. The Bible employs this term when it describes the human life.

Let us note here that the words "soul" and "soul life" in the Bible are one and the same in the original. In the Old

7

Testament the Hebrew word for "soul"—*nephesh*—is used equally for "soul life." The New Testament consequently employs the Greek word *psuche* for both "soul" and "soul life." Hence we know "soul" not only is one of the three elements of man but also is man's life, his natural life. In many places in the Bible, "soul" is translated as "life."

Inasmuch as we have seen how soul is the site of our personality, the organ of volition and the natural life, we can easily conclude that this soul is also the "real I"—I myself. Our self is the soul. This too can be demonstrated by the Bible. In Numbers 30, the phrase "bind himself" occurs ten times. In the original it is "bind his soul." From this we are led to understand that the soul is our own self. In many other passages of the Bible we find the word "soul" is translated as "self."

THE FALL OF MAN

For the wages of sin is death, but the free gift of God is eternal life in Christ Jesus our Lord.

Romans 6.23 (NASV)

The man God fashioned was notably different from all other created beings. Man possessed a spirit similar to that of the angels and at the same time had a soul resembling that of the lower animals. When God created man He gave him a perfect freedom. He did not make man an automaton, controlled automatically by His will. This is evident in Genesis 2 at the time God instructed the original man what fruit he could eat and what not. The man God created was not a machine run by God; instead he had perfect freedom of choice. If he chose to obey God, he could; if he decided to rebel against God, he could do that too. Man had in his possession a sovereignty by which he could exercise his volition in choosing to obey or to disobey. This is a most important point, for we must realize that in our spiritual life God never deprives us our freedom. Unless we actively cooperate, God will not undertake anything for us. Neither God nor the devil can do any work without first obtaining our consent, for man's will is free.

Man's spirit was originally the highest part of his entire being to which soul and body were to be subject. Under normal conditions the spirit is like a mistress, the soul like a steward, and the body like a servant. The mistress commits matters to the steward who in turn commands the servant to carry them out. The mistress gives orders privately to the steward; the steward in turn transmits them openly to the servant. The steward appears to be the lord of all, but in actuality the lord over all is the mistress. Unfortunately man has fallen; he has been defeated and has sinned;

consequently, the proper order of spirit, soul, and body has been confused.

God bestowed upon man a sovereign power and accorded numerous gifts to a human soul. Thought and will or intellect and intention are among the prominent portions. The original purpose of God is that the human soul should receive and assimilate the truth and substance of God's spiritual life. He gave gifts to men in order that man might take God's knowledge and will as his own. If man's spirit and soul would maintain their created perfection, healthiness and liveliness, his body would then be able to continue forever without change. If he would exercise his will by taking and eating the fruit of life, God's Own life undoubtedly would enter his spirit, permeate his soul, transform his entire inner man, and translate his body into incorruptibility. He then would literally be in possession of "eternal life." In that event his soulical life would be filled completely with spiritual life, and his whole being would be transformed into that which is spiritual. Conversely, if the order of spirit and soul would be reversed, then man would plunge into darkness and the human body could not last long but would soon be corrupted.

We know how man's soul chose the tree of the knowledge of good and evil rather than the tree of life. Yet is it not clear that God's will for Adam was to eat the fruit of the tree of life? Because before He forbade Adam to eat the fruit of the tree of good and evil and warned him that in the day he ate he should die (Genesis 2.17), He first commanded man to eat freely of every tree of the garden and purposely mentioned the tree of life in the midst of the garden. Who can say that this is not so?

"The fruit of the knowledge of good and evil" uplifts the human soul and suppresses the spirit. God does not forbid man to eat of this fruit merely to test man. He forbids it because He knows that by eating this fruit man's soul life will be so stimulated that his spirit life will be stifled. This means man will lose the true knowledge of God and thus be dead to Him.

God's forbiddance shows God's love. The knowledge of good and evil in this world is itself evil. Such knowledge springs from the intellect of man's soul. It puffs up the soul life and consequently deflates the spirit life to the point of losing any knowledge of God, to the point of becoming as much as dead.

A great number of God's servants view this tree of life as God offering life to the world in His Son the Lord Jesus. This is eternal life, God's nature, His uncreated life. Hence, we have here two trees—one germinates spiritual life while the other develops soulish life. Man in his original state is neither sinful nor holy and righteous. He stands between the two. Either he can accept God's life, thus becoming a spiritual man and a partaker of divine nature; or he can inflate his created life into becoming soulish, consequently inflicting death on his spirit. God imparted a perfect balance to the three parts of man. Whenever one part is over-developed the others are afflicted.

In examining the nature of Adam's sin we discover that aside from rebellion there is also a certain kind of independence. We must not lose sight here of free will. On the one hand, the tree of life implies a sense of *dependence*. Man at that time did not possess God's nature, but had he partaken of the fruit of the tree of life he could have secured God's life; man could have reached his summit—possessing the very life of God. This is dependence. On the other hand, the tree of the knowledge of good and evil suggests *independence* because man strived by the exercise of his will for the knowledge not promised, for something not accorded him by God. His rebellion declared his independence. By rebelling he did not need to depend upon God. Furthermore, his seeking the knowledge of good and evil also showed his independence, for he was not satisfied with what God had bestowed already. The difference between the spiritual and the soulish is crystal clear. The spiritual depends utterly upon God, fully satisfied with what God has given; the soulish steers clear of God and covets what God has not conferred, especially "knowledge." Independence is a special mark of the soulish. That thing—no matter how good, even worshiping God—is unquestionably of the soul if it does not require complete trust in God and instead calls for reliance upon one's own strength. The tree of life cannot grow within us together with the tree of knowledge. Rebellion and independence explain every sin committed by both sinners and saints.

SPIRIT, SOUL, AND BODY AFTER THE FALL

Adam lived by the breath of life becoming spirit in him. By the spirit he sensed God, knew God's voice, and communed with God. He had a very keen awareness of God. But after his fall his spirit died.

When God spoke to Adam at the first He said, "in the day that you eat of it (the fruit of the tree of good and evil) you shall die" (Genesis 2.17). Adam and Eve nevertheless continued on for hundreds of years after eating the forbidden fruit. This obviously indicates that the death God foretold was not physical. Adam's death began in his spirit.

What really is death? According to its scientific definition, death is "the cessation of communication with environment." Death of the spirit is the cessation of its communication with God. Death of the body is the cutting off of communication between spirit and body. So when we say the spirit is dead it does not imply there is no more spirit; we simply mean the spirit has lost its sensitivity towards God and thus is dead to Him. The exact situation is that the spirit is incapacitated, unable to commune with God. To illustrate. A dumb person has a mouth and lungs but something is wrong with his vocal cords and he is powerless to speak. So far as human language is concerned his mouth may be considered dead. Similarly Adam's spirit died because of his disobedience to God. He still had his spirit, yet it was dead to God for it had lost its spiritual instinct. It is still so; sin has destroyed the spirit's keen intuitive knowledge of God and rendered man spiritually dead. He may be religious, moral, learned, capable, strong and wise, but he is dead to God. He may even talk about God, reason about God and preach God, but he is still dead to Him. Man is not able to hear or to sense the voice of God's Spirit. Consequently in the New Testament God often refers to those who are living in the flesh as dead.

The death which began in our forefather's spirit gradually spread until it reached his body. Though he lived on for many years after his spirit was dead, death nevertheless worked incessantly in him until his spirit, soul, and body were all dead. His body, which could have been transformed and glorified, was instead returned to dust. Because his inward man had fallen into chaos, his outward body must die and be destroyed.

Henceforth Adam's spirit (as well as the spirit of all his descendants) fell under the oppression of the soul until it gradually merged with the soul and the two parts became closely united. The writer of Hebrews declares in 4.12 that the Word of God shall pierce and divide soul and spirit. The dividing is necessary because spirit and soul have become one. While they are intimately knit they plunge man into a psychic world. Everything is done according to the dictates of intellect or feeling. The spirit has lost its power and sensation, as though dead asleep. What instinct it has in knowing and serving God is entirely paralyzed. It remains in a coma as if non-existent. This is what is meant in Jude 19 by "natural, not having spirit" (literal).This certainly does not mean the human spirit ceases to exist, for Numbers 16.22 distinctly states that God is "the God of the spirits of all flesh." Every human being still has in his possession a spirit, although it is darkened by sin and impotent to hold communion with God.

In yielding to the demand of its passions and lusts the soul has become a slave to the body so that the Holy Spirit finds it useless to strive for God's place in such a one. Hence the Scripture declares, "My Spirit shall not always plead with

Man; for he indeed is flesh" (Genesis 6.3 Darby). The Bible refers to the flesh as the composite of the unregenerated soul and the physical life, though more often than not it points to sin which is in the body. Once man is completely under the dominion of the flesh he has no possibility of liberating himself. Soul has replaced the spirit's authority. Everything is done independently and according to the dictates of his mind. Even in religious matters, in the hottest pursuit of God, all is carried on by the strength and will of man's soul, void of the Holy Spirit's revelation. The soul is not merely independent of the spirit; it is additionally under the body's control. It is now asked to obey, to execute and to fulfill the lusts, passions and demands of the body. Every son of Adam is therefore not only dead in his spirit but he is also "from the earth, a man of dust" (1 Corinthians 15.47). Fallen men are governed completely by the flesh, walking in response to the desires of their soulish life and physical passions. Such ones are unable to commune with God. Sometimes they display their intellect, at other times their passion, but more other both their intellect and passion. Unimpeded, the flesh is in firm control over the total man.

This is what is unfolded in Jude 18 and 19 — "mockers, walking after their own lusts of ungodlinesses. These are they who set themselves apart, natural men, not having spirit" (Darby). Being soulish is antagonistic to being spiritual. The spirit, that noblest part of us, the part which may be united to God and ought to regulate the soul and body, is now under the dominion of the soul, that part of us which is earthly in both its motive and aim. The spirit has been stripped of its original position. Man's present condition is abnormal. Wherefore he is pictured as not having spirit. The result of being soulish is that he becomes a mocker, pursuing ungodly passions and creating divisions.

First Corinthians 2.14 speaks of such unregenerated persons in this fashion: "The natural (soulish) man does not receive the gifts of the spirit of God, for they are folly to him, and he is not able to understand them because they are spiritually discerned." Such men as are under the control of their souls with their spirits suppressed are in direct contrast to spiritual people. They may be exceedingly intelligent, able to present masterful ideas or theories, yet they do not consent to the things of the Spirit of God. They are unfit to receive revelation from the Holy Spirit. Such revelation is vastly different from human ideas. Man may think human intellect and reasoning are almighty, that the brain is able to comprehend all truths of the world; but the verdict of God's Word is, "vanity of vanities."

God's thought is for the spirit to have the pre-eminence, ruling our soul. But once man turns fleshly his spirit sinks into servitude to the soul. Further degradation follows when man becomes "bodily" (of the body), for the basest body rises to be sovereign. Man has then descended from "spirit-control" to "soul-control," and from "soul-control" to "body-control." Deeper and deeper he sinks. How pitiful it must be when the flesh gains dominion.

Sin has slain the spirit: spiritual death hence becomes the portion of all, for all are dead in sins and trespasses. Sin has rendered the soul independent: the soulish life is therefore but a selfish and self-willed one. Sin has finally empowered the body: sinful nature accordingly reigns through the body.

SALVATION

He (God the Father) made Him (the Son) who knew no sin to be sin on our behalf, so that we might become the righteousness of God in Him.

2 Corinthians 5.21 (NASV)

CALVARY'S JUDGMENT

Death entered the world through the fall of man. Reference here is to spiritual death which separates man from God. Through sin it came in the beginning and so has it ever come since then. Death always comes through sin. Note what Romans 5.12 tells us about this matter. First, that "sin came into the world through one man." Adam sinned and introduced sin into the world. Second, that "death (came into the world) through sin." Death is sin's unchanging result. And lastly, that therefore "death spread to all men because all men sinned." Not merely has death "spread *to*" or "passed *upon*" (Darby) all men, but literally "to all men the death did pass *through*" (Young's). Death has permeated the spirit, soul, and body of all men; there is no part of a human being into which it has not found its way. It is therefore imperative that man receive God's life. The way of salvation cannot be in human reform, for "death" is irreparable. Sin must be judged before there can be rescue out of death. Exactly this is what has been provided by the salvation of the Lord Jesus.

The man who sins must die. This is announced in the Bible. No animal nor angel can suffer the penalty of sin in man's stead. It is man's triune nature which sins, therefore it is man who must die. Only humanity can atone for humanity. But because sin is in his humanity, man's own death cannot atone for his sin. The Lord Jesus came and took human nature upon Himself in order that *He* might be judged instead of humanity.

16

Untainted by sin, His holy human nature could therefore through death atone for sinful humanity. He died a substitute, suffered all penalty of sin, and offered his life a ransom for many. Consequently, whoever believes on Him shall be judged no more (John 5.24).

When the Word became flesh He included all flesh in Himself. As the action of one man, Adam, represents the action of all mankind, so the work of one man, Christ, represents the work of all. We must see how inclusive Christ is before we can understand what redemption is. Why is it that the sin of one man, Adam, is judged to be the sin of all men both present and past? Because Adam is humanity's head from whom all other men have come into the world. Similarly the obedience of one man, Christ, becomes the righteousness of many, both of the present and the past, inasmuch as Christ constitutes the head of a new mankind entered into by a new birth.

Since humanity must be judged, the Son of God—even the man Jesus Christ—suffered in his spirit, soul, and body on the cross for the sins of the world.

Let us first consider his physical sufferings. Man sins through his body and there enjoys the temporary pleasure of sin. The body must accordingly be the recipient of punishment. Who can fathom the physical sufferings of the Lord Jesus on the cross? Are not Christ's sufferings in the body clearly foretold in the Messianic writings? "They have pierced my hands and feet" (Psalm 22.16). The prophet Zechariah called attention to "him whom they have pierced" (12.10). His hands, His feet, His brow, His side, His heart were all pierced by men, pierced *by* sinful humanity and pierced *for* sinful humanity. Many were His wounds and high ran His fever for, with the weight of His whole body hanging unsupported on the cross, His blood could not circulate freely. He was extremely thirsty and therefore cried out, "My tongue cleaves to my jaws"—"for my thirst they gave me vinegar to drink" (Psalm

17

22.15, 69.21). The hands must be nailed, for they love to sin. The mouth must suffer, for it loves to sin. The feet must be pierced, for they love to sin. The brow must be crowned with a thorny crown, for it too loves to sin. All that the human body needed to suffer was executed upon His body. Thus He suffered physically even to death. It was within His power to escape these sufferings, yet He willingly offered His body to endure immeasurable trials and pains, never for a moment shrinking back until He knew that "all was now finished" (John 19.28). Only then did He dismiss His spirit.

Not His body only, His soul as well, suffered. The soul is the organ of self-consciousness. Before being crucified, Christ was administered wine mingled with myrrh as a sedative to alleviate pain, but He refused it as He was not willing to lose His consciousness. Human souls have fully enjoyed the pleasure of sins; accordingly in His soul Jesus would endure the pain of sins. He would rather drink the cup given Him by God than the cup which numbed consciousness.

How shameful is the punishment of the cross! It was used to execute runaway slaves. A slave had neither property nor rights. His body belonged to his master; he could therefore be punished with the most shameful cross. The Lord Jesus took the place of a slave and was crucified. Isaiah called Him "the servant"; Paul said He took the form of a slave. Yes, as a slave He came to rescue us who are subject to the lifelong bondage of sin and Satan. We are slaves to passion, temper, habits and the world. We are sold to sin. Yet He died because of our slavery and bore our entire shame.

The Bible records that the soldiers took the garments of the Lord Jesus (John 19.23). He was nearly naked when crucified. This is one of the shames of the cross. Sin takes our radiant garment away and renders us naked. Our Lord was stripped bare before Pilate and again on Calvary. How would His holy soul react to such abuse? Would it not insult the holiness of His personality and cover Him with shamefulness? Who can enter into His feeling of that tragic moment? Because every man had enjoyed the apparent glory of sin, so the Savior must endure the real shame of sin. Truly "thou (God) hast covered him with shame . . . with which thy enemies taunt, O Lord, with which they mock the footsteps of thy anointed"; He nonetheless "endured the cross, despising the shame" (Psalm 89.45, 51; Hebrews 12.2).

No one can ever ascertain how fully the soul of the Savior suffered on the cross. We often contemplate His physical suffering but overlook the feeling of His soul. A week before the Passover He was heard to mention: "Now is my soul troubled" (John 12.27). This points to the cross. While in the Garden of Gethsemane Jesus was again heard to say: "My soul is very sorrowful, even to death" (Matthew 26.38). Were it not for these words we would hardly think his soul had suffered. Isaiah 53 mentions thrice how His soul was made an offering for sin, how His soul travailed, and how He poured out His soul to death (vv.10-12). Because Jesus bore the curse and shame of the cross, whoever believes in Him shall no more be cursed and put to shame.

His spirit too suffered immensely. The spirit is that part of man which equips him to commune with God. The Son of God was holy, blameless, unstained, separated from sinners. His spirit was united with the Holy Spirit in perfect oneness. Never did there exist a moment of disturbance and doubt, for He always had God's presence with Him. "It is not I alone," declared Jesus, "but I and he who sent me ... And he who sent me is with me" (John 8.16, 29). For this reason He could pray, "Father, I thank thee that thou hast heard me. I knew that thou hearest me always" (John 11.41-42). Nevertheless, while He hung on the cross—and if there ever were a day when the Son of God desperately needed the presence of God it must be that day—He cried out, "My God, my God, why hast thou forsaken me?" (Matthew 27.46). His spirit was split asunder from God. How intensely He felt the loneliness, the desertion, the separation. The Son was still yielding, the Son was still obeying the will of the Father-God, yet the Son was forsaken: not for His Own sake, but for the sake of others.

Sin affects most deeply the spirit; consequently, holy as the Son of God was, still He had to be wrenched away from the Father because He bore the sin of others. It is true that in the countless days of eternity past "I and the Father are one" (John 10.30). Even during His days of earthly sojourn this remained true, for *His* humanity could not be a cause of separation from God. Sin alone could separate: even though that sin be the sin of others. Jesus suffered this spiritual separation for us in order that our spirit could return to God.

When He surveyed the death of Lazarus, Jesus might have been thinking of His Own approaching death, and so "he was deeply moved in spirit and troubled" (John 11.33). Upon announcing that He would be betrayed and die on the cross, He was again "troubled in spirit" (John 13.21). This tells us why, when He received God's judgment on Calvary, He cried out: "My God, my God, why hast thou forsaken me?" For "I think of God and I moan; I meditate, and my spirit faints" (Matthew 27.46 echoing Psalm 22.1; Psalm 77.3). He was deprived of the mighty strengthening through the Holy Spirit in His spirit (Ephesians 3.16) because His spirit was torn away from the Spirit of God. Therefore He sighed, "I am poured out like water, and all my bones are out of joint; my heart is like wax, it is melted within my breast; my strength is dried up like a potsherd, and my tongue cleaves to my jaws; thou dost lay me in the dust of death" (Psalm 22.14-15).

On the one side, the Holy Spirit of God deserted Him; on the other, the evil spirit of Satan mocked him. It seems apparent that Psalm 22.11-13 refers to this phase: "Be not far from me . . . there is none to help. Many bulls encompass me, strong bulls of Bashan surround me; they opened wide their mouths at me, like a ravening and roaring lion."

His spirit endured God's desertion on the one side and

resisted the evil spirit's derision on the other. Man's human spirit has so separated itself from God, exalted itself, and followed the evil spirit that man's spirit must be totally broken in order that it may no longer resist God and remain allied with the enemy. The Lord Jesus became sin for us on the cross. His inner holy humanity was completely smashed as God passed judgment upon unholy humanity. Forsaken by God, Christ thus suffered sin's bitterest pain, enduring in darkness the punitive wrath of God on sin without the support of the love of God or the light of His countenance. To be forsaken by God is the consequence of sin.

Now our sinful humanity has been judged completely because it was judged in the sinless humanity of the Lord Jesus. In Him, holy humanity has won its victory. Whatever judgment should come upon the body, soul and spirit of sinners has been poured upon Him. He is our representative. By faith we are joined to Him. His death is reckoned as our death, and His judgment as our judgment. Our spirit, soul, and body have altogether been judged and penalized in Him. It would not be any different had we been punished in person. "There is therefore now no condemnation for those who are in Christ Jesus" (Romans 8.1).

This is what He has accomplished for us and such is now our standing before God. "For he who has died is freed from sin" (Romans 6.7). Positionally we already have died in the Lord Jesus; it only awaits the Holy Spirit to translate this fact into our experience. The cross is where the sinner—spirit, soul, and body—is altogether judged. It is through the death and resurrection of the Lord that the Holy Spirit of God is able to impart God's nature to us. The cross bears the sinner's judgment, proclaims the sinner's worthlessness, crucifies the sinner, and releases the life of the Lord Jesus. Henceforth anyone who accepts the cross shall be born anew by the Holy Spirit and receive the life of the Lord Jesus.

LESSON FIVE

THE FLESH AND SALVATION

Those who belong to Christ Jesus have crucified the flesh with its passions and desires.

Galatians 5.24

The word "flesh" is *basar* in Hebrew and *sarx* in Greek. Seen often in the Bible, it is used in various ways. Its most significant usage, observed and made most clear in Paul's writings, has reference to the unregenerated person. Speaking of his old "I," he says in Romans 7: "I am fleshly" (v.14 Darby). Not merely his nature or a particular part of his being is fleshly; the "I"—Paul's whole being—is fleshly. He reiterates this thought in verse 18 by asserting "within me, that is, in my flesh." It follows clearly that "flesh" in the Bible points to all an unregenerated person is. In connection with this usage of "flesh" it must be remembered that in the very beginning man was constituted spirit, soul, and body. As it is the site of man's personality and consciousness, the soul is connected to the spiritual world through man's spirit. The soul must decide whether it is to obey the spirit and hence be united with God and His will or is to yield to the body and all the temptations of the material world. On the occasion of man's fall the soul resisted the spirit's authority and became enslaved to the body and its passions. Thus man became a fleshly, not a spiritual, man. Man's spirit was denied its noble position and was reduced to that of a prisoner. Since the soul is now under the power of the flesh, the Bible deems man to be fleshly or carnal. Whatever is soulical has become fleshly.

THE UNREGENERATED MAN

The Lord Jesus has stated that any unregenerated person born but once (i.e., born only of man), is flesh and is therefore

22

living in the realm of the flesh. During the period we were unregenerated we indeed "lived in the passions of our flesh, following the desires of body and mind, and so we were by nature children of wrath, like the rest of mankind" because "it is not the children of the flesh who are the children of God" (Ephesians 2.3; Romans 9.8). A man whose soul may yield to the lusts of the body and commit many unmentionable sins may be so dead to God (Ephesians 2.1)—"dead in trespasses and the uncircumcision of . . . flesh" (Colossians 2.13)—that he may have no consciousness of being sinful. On the contrary he may even be proud, considering himself better than others. Frankly speaking, "while we were living in the flesh, our sinful passions, aroused by the law, were at work in our members to bear fruit for death" for the simple reason that we were "carnal, sold under sin." We therefore with our flesh "serve the law of sin" (Romans 7.5, 14, 25).

Although the flesh is exceedingly strong in sinning and following selfish desire it is extremely weak towards the will of God. Unregenerated man is powerless to fulfill any of God's will, being "weakened by the flesh." And the flesh is even "hostile to God; it does not submit to God's law, indeed it cannot" (Romans 8.3, 7). This however does not imply that the flesh totally disregards the things of God. The fleshly sometimes do exert their utmost strength to observe the law. The Bible moreover never treats the fleshly as synonymous with the law-breakers. It merely concludes that "by works of the law shall no flesh be justified" (Galatians 2.16 ASV). For the fleshly not to keep the law is certainly nothing unusual. It simply proves they are of the flesh. But now that God has ordained that man shall not be justified by works of law but by faith in the Lord Jesus (Romans 3.28), those who attempt to follow the law only disclose their disobedience to God, seeking to establish their own righteousness in lieu of God's righteousness (Romans 10.3). It reveals further that they belong to the flesh. To sum up, "those who are in the flesh cannot please God" (Romans 8.8), and *this* "cannot" seals the fate of the fleshly.

God looks upon the flesh as utterly corrupt. So closely is it linked with lust that the Bible often refers to "the lusts of the flesh" (2 Peter 2.18 Darby). Great though His power, God nonetheless cannot transform the nature of the flesh into something pleasing to Himself. God Himself declares: "My spirit shall not always strive in man forever, for he is flesh" (Genesis 6.3 Young's). The corruption of the flesh is such that even the Holy Spirit of God cannot by striving against the flesh render it unfleshly. That which is born of the flesh is flesh. Man unfortunately does not understand God's Word and so he tries continually to refine and reform his flesh. Yet the Word of God stands forever. Due to its exceeding corruption, God warns His saints to hate "even the garment spotted by the flesh" (Jude 23).

Because God appreciates the actual condition of the flesh He declares it is unchangeable. Any person who attempts to repair it by acts of self-abasement or severity to the body shall fail utterly. God recognizes the impossibility of the flesh to be changed, improved or bettered. In saving the world, therefore, He does not try to alter man's flesh; He instead gives man a new life in order to help put it to death. The flesh must die. This is salvation.

God's reaction to the sinfulness of all men is to take upon Himself the task of salvation. His way is in "sending his own Son in the likeness of sinful flesh." His Son is without sin, hence He alone is qualified to save us. "In the likeness of sinful flesh" describes His incarnation: how He takes a human body and links Himself with mankind. God's only Son is referred to elsewhere as "the Word" that "became flesh" (John 1.14). His coming in the likeness of sinful flesh is the "became flesh" of that verse. Therefore our verse in Romans 8.3 tells us as well in what manner the Word became flesh. The emphasis here is that He is the Son of God, consequently sinless. Even when He comes in the flesh, Gods' Son does not become "sinful flesh." He only comes in "the *likeness* of sinful flesh." While in the flesh, He remains as the Son of God and is still without sin. Yet because He possesses the likeness of sinful flesh, He is most closely joined with the world's sinners who live in the flesh.

What then is the purpose of His incarnation? As a "sacrifice for sins" is the Biblical explanation (Hebrews 10.12), and this is the work of the cross. God's Son is to atone for our sins. All the fleshly sin against the law; they cannot establish the righteousness of God; and they are doomed to perdition and punishment. But the Lord Jesus in coming to the world takes this likeness of sinful flesh and joins Himself so perfectly with the fleshly that they have been punished for their sin in His death on the cross. He need not suffer for He is without sin, yet He does suffer because He has the likeness of sinful flesh. In the position of a new federal head, the Lord Jesus now includes all sinners in His suffering. This explains the punishment for sin.

Christ as the sacrifice for sin suffers for everyone who is in the flesh. But what about the power of sin which fills the fleshly? "He condemned sin in the flesh." He who is sinless is made sin for us, so that He dies for sin. He is "put to death in the flesh" (1 Peter 3.18). When He dies in the flesh, He takes to the cross the sin in the flesh. This is what is meant by the phrase "condemned sin in the flesh." To condemn is to judge or to mete out punishment. The judgment and punishment of sin is death. Thus the Lord Jesus actually put sin to death in His flesh. We therefore can see in His death that not only our *sins* are judged but *sin itself* is even judged. Henceforth sin has no power upon those who are joined to the Lord's death and who accordingly have sin condemned in their flesh.

THE CONFLICT BETWEEN THE OLD AND THE NEW

It is essential for a regenerated person to understand what

he has obtained through new birth and what still lingers of his natural endowment. Such knowledge will help him as he continues his spiritual journey. It may prove helpful at this point to explain how much is included in man's flesh and likewise how the Lord Jesus in His redemption deals with the constituents of that flesh. In other words, what does a believer inherit in regeneration?

A reading of several verses in Romans 7 can make clear that the components of the flesh are mainly "sin" and "me": "sin that dwells in me . . . , that is, in my flesh" (vv. 14,17-18 Darby). The "sin" here is the power of sin, and the "me" here is what we commonly acknowledge as "self." If a believer would understand spiritual life he must not be confused about these two elements of the flesh.

We know the Lord Jesus has dealt with the sin of our flesh on His cross. And the Word informs us that "our old self was crucified with him" (Romans 6.6). Nowhere in the Bible are we told to be crucified since this has been done and done perfectly by Christ already. With regard to the question of sin, man is not required to do anything. He need only consider this an accomplished fact (Romans 6.11) and he will reap the effectiveness of the death of Jesus in being wholly delivered from the power of sin (Romans 6.14).

We are never asked in the Bible to be crucified for sin, that is true. It *does* exhort us, however, to take up the cross for denying self. The Lord Jesus instructs us many times to deny ourselves and take up the cross and follow Him. The explanation for this is that the Lord Jesus deals with our sins and with ourselves very differently. To wholly conquer sin the believer needs but a moment; to deny the self he needs an entire lifetime. Only on the cross did Jesus *bear* our sins; yet throughout His life the Lord *denied* Himself. The same must be true of us.

The Galatian letter of Paul delineates the relationship between the flesh and the believer. He tells us on the one hand that "those who belong to Christ Jesus have crucified the flesh with its passions and desires" (5.24). On the very day one becomes identified with the Lord Jesus then his flesh also is crucified. Now one might think, without the Holy Spirit's instruction, that his flesh is no longer present, for has it not been crucified? But no, on the other hand the letter says to us to "walk by the Spirit, and do not gratify the desires of the flesh. For the desires of the flesh are against the Spirit, and the desires of the Spirit are against the flesh" (5.16-17). Here we are told openly that one who belongs to Christ Jesus and has already the indwelling Holy Spirit still has the flesh in him. Not only does the flesh exist; it is described as being singularly powerful as well.

What can we say? Are these two Biblical references contradictory? No, verse 24 stresses the sin of the flesh, while verse 17 the self of the flesh. The cross of Christ deals with sin and the Holy Spirit through the cross treats of (deals with) self. Christ delivers the believer completely from the power of sin through the cross that sin may not reign again; but by the Holy Spirit Who dwells in the believer, Christ enables him to overcome self daily and obey Him perfectly. Liberation from sin is an accomplished fact; denial of self is to be a daily experience.

LESSON SIX

THE FLESHLY OR CARNAL BELIEVER

For I, brethren, could not address you as spiritual men, but as men of the flesh, as babes in Christ.

1 Corinthians 3.1

Here the Apostle divides all Christians into two classes: the spiritual and the fleshly or carnal. The spiritual Christians are not at all extraordinary; they are simply normal. It is the fleshly who are out of the ordinary, because they are abnormal. Those at Corinth were indeed Christians, but they were fleshly, not spiritual. Three times in this chapter Paul declares they were men of the flesh. Through the wisdom given him by the Holy Spirit the Apostle was made to realize that he first must identify them before he could offer them the message they needed.

Biblical regeneration is a birth by which the innermost part of man's being, the deeply hidden spirit, is renewed and indwelt by the Spirit of God. It requires time for the power of this new life to reach the outside: that is, to be extended from the center to the circumference. Hence we cannot expect to find the strength of "the young men" nor the experience of "the fathers" manifested in the life of a child in Christ. Although a newly born believer may proceed faithfully, loving the Lord best and distinguishing himself in zeal, he still needs time for opportunities to know more of the wickedness of sin and self and occasions to know more of the will of God and the way of the spirit. However much he may love the Lord or love the truth, this new believer still walks in the realm of feelings and thoughts, not yet having been tested and refined by fire. A newly born Christian cannot help being fleshly. Though filled with the Holy Spirit, he nevertheless does not know the flesh. How can one be liberated from the works of the flesh if he does not recognize that such works

28

spring from the flesh? In assessing their actual condition, therefore, newly born babes are generally of the flesh.

The Bible does not expect new Christians to be spiritual instantaneously; if they should remain as babes after many years, however, then their situation is indeed most pitiful. Paul himself points out to the Corinthians that he had treated them as men of the flesh earlier because they were new born babes in Christ, and that by now—at the moment of his writing them—they certainly should be growing into manhood. They had instead frittered away their lives, remained as babes, and were thus still fleshly.

What are the characteristics of the fleshly? Foremost among them is remaining long as babes. The duration of babyhood should not exceed a few years. When one is born anew by believing that the Son of God atoned for his sins on the cross, he simultaneously ought to believe that he has been crucified with Christ in order that the Holy Spirit may release him from the power of the flesh. Ignorance of this naturally will keep him in the flesh for many years.

The second characteristic of the fleshly is that they are unfit to absorb spiritual teaching. "I fed you with milk, not solid food; for you were not ready." The Corinthians grossly prided themselves on their knowledge and wisdom. Of all the churches in that period, that at Corinth was probably the most informed one. Paul early in his letter thanked God for their rich knowledge (1 Corinthians 1.5). Should Paul deliver spiritual sermons to them they could understand every word; however, all their understandings were in the mind. Although they knew everything, these Corinthians did not have the power to express in life that which they knew. Most likely there are many fleshly believers today who grasp so much so well that they can even preach to others but who are themselves yet unspiritual. Genuine spiritual knowledge lies not in wonderful and mysterious thoughts but in actual spiritual experience through union of the believer's life with truth. Cleverness is useless here, while eagerness for truth is insufficient too; the *sine qua non* (absolutely indispensable thing) is a path of perfect obedience to the Holy Spirit Who alone truly teaches us. All else is merely the transmission of knowledge from one mind to another. Such data will not render a fleshly person spiritual; on the contrary, his carnal walk actually will turn all his "spiritual" knowledge into that which is fleshly. What he needs is not increased spiritual teaching but an obedient heart which is willing to yield his life to the Holy Spirit and go the way of the cross according to the Spirit's command. Increased spiritual teaching will only strengthen his carnality and serve to deceive him into conceiving himself as spiritual. For does he not say to himself, "How else could I possibly know so many spiritual things unless I were spiritual?" Whereas the real touchstone should be, "How much do you truly know from life or is it merely a product of the mind?" May God be gracious to us.

Paul wrote of yet another evidence of being fleshly when he affirmed that "while there is jealousy and strife among you, are you not of the flesh, and behaving like ordinary men?" The sin of jealousy and strife is eminent proof of carnality. Dissensions were rife in the church at Corinth, as is confirmed by such declarations as "I belong to Paul," "I belong to Apollos," "I belong to Cephas," "I belong to Christ" (1 Corinthians 1.12). Even those who were contending for Christ by saying "I am of Christ" were included among the fleshly, for the spirit of flesh is always and everywhere jealous and contentious. For these to hold themselves up as being of Christ, but in that attitude of spirit, is inescapably carnal. However sweet the word may sound, any sectarian boasting is but the babbling of a babe. The divisions in the church are due to no other cause than to lack of love and walking after the flesh. Such an individual, supposedly contending for the truth, is simply camouflaging the real person. The sinners of the world are men of the flesh; as such, they are not regenerated;

they are therefore under the rule of their soul and body. For a believer to be fleshly signifies that he too is behaving like an ordinary man. Now it is perfectly natural for worldly people to be fleshly; it is understandable if even newly born believers are fleshly; but if, according to the years during which you have believed in the Lord you ought to be spiritual, then how can you continue to behave as an ordinary man?

It is evident that a person belongs to the flesh if he comports himself like an ordinary man and sins often. No matter how much spiritual teaching he knows or how many spiritual experiences he purports to have had or how much effective service he has rendered: none of these makes him less carnal if he remains undelivered from his peculiar temperament, his temper, his selfishness, his contention, his vainglory, his unforgiving or unloving spirit.

To be fleshly or carnal means to behave "like ordinary men." We should ask ourselves whether or not our conduct differs very radically from ordinary men. If many worldly manners cling to your life then you are doubtless still of the flesh. Let us not argue over our being labeled as either spiritual or carnal. If we are not governed by the Holy Spirit what profit will the mere designation of spiritual be to us? This is after all a matter of life, not of title.

THE THINGS OF THE FLESH

The flesh has many outlets. We have learned how it is hostile to God and cannot possibly please Him. Neither believer nor sinner, however, can genuinely appreciate the complete worthlessness, wickedness, and defilement of the flesh as viewed by God unless he is shown by the Holy Spirit. Only when God by His Spirit has revealed to man the true condition of the flesh as God sees it will man then deal with his flesh.

The manifestations of the flesh manward are well-known. If a person is strict with himself and refuses to follow, as he once did, "the desires of body and mind" (Ephesians 2.3), he will detect easily how defiled are these manifestations. The Galatian letter of Paul gives a list of these sins of the flesh so that none can be mistaken—"Now the works of the flesh are plain: immorality, impurity, licentiousness, idolatry, sorcery, enmity, strife, jealousy, anger, selfishness, dissension, party spirit (literally, "sect"), envy, drunkenness, carousing, and the like" (5.19-21). In this enumeration the Apostle declares that "the works of the flesh are plain." Whoever is willing to understand certainly shall recognize them. To ascertain whether one is of the flesh, he need but inquire of himself if he is doing any of these works of the flesh. It is of course unnecessary for him to commit all in the list in order to be carnal. Were he to do merely one of them he would establish himself beyond doubt as being fleshly, for how could he do any one of them if the flesh had relinquished its rule already? The presence of a work of the flesh proves the existence of the flesh.

These works of the flesh may be divided into five groups: (1) sins which defile the body, such as immorality, impurity, licentiousness; (2) sinful supernatural communications with satanic forces, such as idolatry, sorcery; (3) sinful temper and its peculiarities, such as enmity, strife, jealousy, anger; (4) religious sects and parties, such as selfishness, dissensions, party spirit, envy; and (5) lasciviousness, such as drunkenness and carousing. Every one of these is easily observed. Those who do them are of the flesh.

THE CROSS AND THE HOLY SPIRIT

For if you are living according to the flesh, you must die; but if by the Spirit you are putting to death the deeds of the body, you will live.

Romans 8.13 (NASV)

Upon reciting many deeds of the flesh in his Galatian letter, the Apostle Paul then points out that "those who belong to Christ Jesus have crucified the flesh with its passions and desires" (Galatians 5.24). Here is deliverance. Is it not strange that what concerns the believer vastly differs from what concerns God? The former is concerned with "the works of the flesh" (Galatians 5.19), that is, with the varying sins of the flesh. He is occupied with today's anger, tomorrow's jealousy, or the day after tomorrow's strife. The believer mourns over a particular sin and longs for victory over it. Yet all these sins are but fruits from the same tree. While plucking one fruit (actually one cannot pick off any), out crops another. One after another they grow, giving him no chance for victory. On the other hand God is concerned not with the *works* of the flesh but with "the flesh" itself (Galatians 5.24). Had the tree been put to death, would there be any need to fear lest it bear fruit? The believer busily makes plans to handle sins—which are the fruits, while forgetting to deal with the flesh itself—which is the root. No wonder that before he can clear up one sin, another has burst forth. We must therefore deal today with the source of sin.

Babes in Christ need to appropriate the deeper meaning of the cross, for they are still carnal. The aim of God is to crucify the believer's old man with Christ with the result that they who belong to Christ "have crucified the flesh with its passions and desires." Bear in mind that it is the flesh together with its powerful passions and desires that has been crucified. As the

33

sinner was regenerated and redeemed from his sins through the cross, so now the carnal babe in Christ must be delivered from the rule of the flesh by the same cross so that he can walk according to the Spirit and no longer according to the flesh. Thereafter it will not be long before he becomes a spiritual Christian.

It may be helpful to be more explicit here. We have indicated that the crucifixion of the flesh is not dependent upon experiences, however different they may be; rather is it contingent upon the fact of God's finished work. "Those who belong to Christ Jesus"—the weak as well as the strong—"have crucified the flesh with its passions and desires." You say you still sin, but God says you have been crucified on the cross. You say your temper persists, but God's answer is that you have been crucified. You say your lusts remain very potent, but again God replies that your flesh has been crucified on the cross. For the moment will you please not look at your experience, but just hearken to what God says to you. If you do not listen to His Word and instead look daily upon your situation, you will never enter into the reality of your flesh having been crucified on the cross. Disregard your feelings and experience. God pronounces your flesh crucified; it therefore *has* been crucified. Simply respond to God's Word and you shall have experience. When God tells you that "your flesh has been crucified" you should answer with "Amen, indeed my flesh has been crucified." In thus acting upon His Word you shall see your flesh is dead indeed.

THE HOLY SPIRIT AND EXPERIENCE

"While we were living in the flesh, our sinful passions . . . were at work in our members to bear fruit for death. But now we are . . . dead. . ." (Romans 7.5-6). Because of this the flesh has no rule over us any further.

We have believed and acknowledged that our flesh has been crucified on the cross. *Now*—not before—we can turn our attention to the matter of experience. Though we presently stress experience, we nevertheless firmly hold to the fact of our crucifixion with Christ. What God has done for us and what we experience of God's completed work, though distinguishable, are inseparable.

God has done what He could do. The question next is, what attitude do we assume towards His finished work? Not just in name but in actuality has He crucified our flesh on the cross. If we believe and if we exercise our will to choose what God has accomplished for us, it will become our life experience. We are not asked to do anything because God has done it all. We are not required to crucify our flesh for God has crucified it on the cross. Do you believe this is true? Do you desire to possess it in your life? If we believe and if we desire then we shall cooperate with the Holy Spirit in obtaining rich experience. Colossians 3.5 implores us to "put to death therefore what is earthly in you." This is the path towards experience. The "therefore" indicates the consequence of what precedes it in verse 3; namely, "you have died." The "you have died" is what God has achieved for us. Because "you have died," therefore "put to death what is earthly in you." The first mention of death here is our factual position in Christ; the second, our actual experience. The failure of believers today can be traced to a failure to see the relationship between these two deaths. Some have attempted to put their flesh to nought for they lay stress only upon the death experience. Their flesh consequently grows livelier with each dealing! Others have acknowledged the truth that their flesh in fact was crucified with Christ on the cross; yet they do not seek the practical reality of it. Neither of these can ever appropriate experimentally the crucifixion of the flesh.

If we desire to put our members to death we first must have a ground for such action; otherwise we merely rely upon our strength. No degree of zeal can ever bring the desired experience to us. Moreover, if we only know our flesh has been crucified with Christ but are not exercised to have His accomplished work carried out in us, our knowledge too will be unavailing. A putting to nought requires a knowing first of an identification in His death; knowing our identification, we must exercise the putting to death. These two must go together. We are deceiving ourselves should we be satisfied with just perceiving the fact of identification, thinking we are now spiritual because the flesh has been destroyed; on the other hand, it is an equal deception if in putting to nought the wicked deeds of the flesh we over-emphasize *them* and fail to take a death attitude towards the flesh. Should we forget that the flesh is dead we shall never be able to lay anything to rest. The "put to death" is contingent upon the "you have died." This putting to death means bringing the death of the Lord Jesus to bear upon all the deeds of the flesh. The crucifixion of the Lord is a most authoritative one for it puts away everything it encounters. Since we are united with Him in His crucifixion we can apply His death to any member which is tempted to lust and immediately put it to nought.

Our union with Christ in His death signifies that it is an accomplished fact in our spirits. What a believer must do now is to bring this sure death out of his spirit and apply it to his members each time his wicked lusts may be aroused. Such spiritual death is not a once for all proposition. Whenever the believer is not watchful or loses his faith, the flesh will certainly go on a rampage. If he desires to be conformed completely to the Lord's death, he must unceasingly put to nought the deeds of his members so that what is real in the spirit may be executed in the body.

But whence comes the power to so apply the crucifixion of the Lord to our members? It is "by the Spirit," insists Paul, that "you put to death the deeds of the body" (Romans 8.13). To put away these deeds the believer must rely upon the Holy Spirit to translate his co-crucifixion with Christ into personal experience. He must believe that the Holy Spirit will

THE CROSS AND THE HOLY SPIRIT

administer the death of the cross on whatever needs to die. In view of the fact that the believer's flesh was crucified with Christ on the cross, he does not need today to be crucified once again. All which is required is to apply, by the Holy Spirit, the accomplished death of the Lord Jesus for him on the cross to any particular wicked deed of the body which now tries to rise up. It will then be put aside by the power of the Lord's death. The wicked works of the flesh may spring up at any time and at any place; accordingly, unless the child of God by the Holy Spirit continually turns to account that power of the holy death of our Lord Jesus, he will not be able to triumph. But if in this way he lays the deeds of the body to rest, the Holy Spirit Who indwells him will ultimately realize God's purpose of putting the body of sin out of a job (Romans 6.6). By thus appropriating the cross the babe in Christ will be liberated from the power of the flesh and will be united with the Lord Jesus in resurrection life.

THE EXISTENCE OF THE FLESH

Let us note carefully that though the flesh may be so put to death that it becomes "ineffective" (the real meaning of "destroy" in Romans 6.6), it endures nonetheless. It is a great error to consider the flesh eradicated from us and to conclude that the nature of sin is completely annihilated. Such false teaching leads people astray. Regenerated life does not alter the flesh; co-crucifixion does not extinguish the flesh; the indwelling Holy Spirit does not render it impossible to walk by the flesh. The flesh with its fleshly nature abides perpetually in the believer. Whenever opportunity is provided for its operation, it at once will spring into action.

LESSON EIGHT

THE BOASTINGS OF THE FLESH

Put no confidence in the flesh.

Philippians 3.3b

The opposition manifested by the flesh against the spirit and against the Holy Spirit is two-fold: (1) by way of committing sin—rebelling against God and breaking the law of God; and (2) by way of performing good—obeying God and following the will of God. The body element of the flesh, full of sin and lust, naturally cannot but express itself in many sins, much to the grief of the Holy Spirit. The soul part of the flesh, however, is not as defiled as the body. Soul is the life principle of man; it is his very self, comprising the faculties of will, mind and emotion. From the human viewpoint the works of the soul may not be all defiled. They merely center upon one's thought, idea, feeling, and like or dislike. Though these all are focused upon self, they are not necessarily defiling sins. The basic characteristic of the works of the soul is independence or self-dependence. Even though the soul side is therefore not as defiled as the body side, it nonetheless is hostile to the Holy Spirit. The flesh makes self the center and elevates self-will above God's will. It may serve God, but always according to its idea, not according to God's. It will do what is good in its own eyes. Self is the principle behind every action. It may not commit what man considers sin: it may even try to keep God's commandments with all its power: yet "self" never fails to be at the heart of every activity. Who can fathom the deceitfulness and vitality of this self? The flesh opposes the spirit not just in sinning against God, but now even in the matter of serving Him and pleasing Him. It opposes and quenches the Holy Spirit by leaning upon its own strength without wholly relying upon God's grace and simply being led by the Spirit.

We can find many believers around us who are by nature good and patient and loving. Now what the believer hates is sin; therefore if he can be delivered from it and from the works of the flesh as described in Galatians 5, verses 19 through 21, then is he content. But what the believer *admires* is righteousness; therefore he will try hard to act righteously, longing to possess the fruits of Galatians 5, verses 22 and 23. Yet, just here lies the danger. For the Christian has not come to learn how to hate the *totality* of his flesh. He merely desires to be liberated from the sins which spring from it. He knows how to resist somewhat the deeds of the flesh, but he does not realize that the entire flesh itself needs to be destroyed. What deceives him is that the flesh not only can produce sin but can also perform good. If it is still doing good it is evident it is yet alive. Had the flesh definitely died the believer's ability both to do good and to do evil would have perished with it. An ability to undertake good manifests that the flesh has not yet died.

Romans 8 maintains that "those who are in the flesh cannot please God" (v.8). It implies that the fleshly have tried, but unsuccessfully, to please God. This of course refers specifically to the righteous acts of the flesh which utterly fail to please God.

The Apostle protests in his Philippian letter that he "put no confidence in the flesh" (3.3). It tends to be self-confident. Because they themselves are so able, the fleshly do not need to trust in the Holy Spirit. Christ crucified is the wisdom of God, but how much confidence a believer reposes in his own wisdom! He can read and preach the Bible, he can hear and believe the Word, but all are executed in the power of his mind, without experiencing the slightest inner registration of a need to depend absolutely upon the instruction of the Holy Spirit. Many therefore believe they possess all the truth, though what they have comes merely from hearing others or from themselves searching the Scriptures. What is of man far exceeds what is of God. They do not have a heart to receive instruction from Him or to wait upon the Lord to reveal to them His truth in His light.

Self-confidence and self-reliance, as we have said, are the notable traits of the good works of the flesh. It is impossible for the flesh to lean upon God. It is too impatient to tolerate any delay. So long as it deems itself strong it will never depend upon God. Even in a time of desperation the flesh continues to scheme and to search for a loophole. It never has the sense of utter dependency. This alone can be a test whereby a believer may know whether or not a work is of the flesh. Whatever does not issue from waiting upon God, from depending upon the Holy Spirit, is unquestionably of the flesh. Whatever one decides according to his pleasure in lieu of seeking the will of God emanates from the flesh. Whenever a heart of utter trust is lacking, there is the labor of the flesh. Now the things done may not be evil or improper; they in fact may be good and godly (such as reading the Bible, praying, worshiping, preaching); but if they are not undertaken in a spirit of complete reliance upon the Holy Spirit, then the flesh is the source of all. The old creation is willing to do anything—even to submit to God—if only it is permitted to live and to be active! However good the deed of the flesh may appear to be, "I," whether veiled or seen, always looms large on the horizon. The flesh never acknowledges its weakness nor admits to its uselessness; even should it become a laughingstock, the flesh remains unshaken in the belief in its ability.

"Having begun with the Spirit, are you now ending with the flesh?" This uncovers a great truth. One may begin well, in the Spirit, but not continue well therein. Our experience bears out the fact of the relative ease with which a thing may begin in the Spirit but end up in the flesh. Often a newly apprehended truth is imparted by the Holy Spirit; after awhile, however, this truth has turned into a boasting of the flesh. The Jews in the early days committed just such an error. How frequently in the matters of obeying the Lord, of denying one's self afresh, of receiving power to save souls, one genuinely may rely upon the Holy Spirit at the outset; yet not long afterwards that same person changes God's grace into his own glory, treating what is of God as his possession. The same principle holds true in our conduct. Through the working of the Holy Spirit at the beginning there occurs a mighty transformation in one's life whereby he loves what he previously hated and hates what he loved before. Gradually, though, "self" begins to creep in unawares. The person increasingly interprets these changes to be of his making and unto his own admiration; or he grows careless and gradually pushes on by self-trust rather than by dependence upon the Holy Spirit. Thousands of matters there are in the experiences of believers which begin well in the Spirit but terminate unfortunately in the flesh.

THE SINS WHICH FOLLOW

Should a believer be so self-confident that he dares to complete the task of the Holy Spirit in the energy of the flesh, he will not come into full spiritual maturity. He will instead drift until the sins he previously had overcome return to him again in power. Do not be surprised by what is said here. It is a spiritual truism that wherever or whenever the flesh is serving God, there and then the power of sin is strengthened. Why did the proud Pharisees become slaves to sin? Was it not because they were too self-righteous and served God too zealously? Why did the Apostle chide the Galatians? Why did they manifest the deeds of the flesh? Was it not because they sought to establish their own righteousness by works and to perfect by the flesh the work which the Holy Spirit had begun? The hazard for young believers is to stop short of the putting to death of the power of the flesh in doing good by only knowing what the cross does for the sinful side of the flesh. In so doing they retreat again into the sins of the flesh. The greatest blunder Christians commit upon experiencing victory over sin lies in not using the way of victory to sustain it; instead they try to perpetuate the victory by their works and determination. It may perhaps succeed for a while. Before long though they shall find themselves sliding back into their former sins, which may differ in form but not in essence. They then either slump into despair by concluding that constant and persistent triumph is impossible to achieve or they try to camouflage their sins without honestly confessing that they have sinned. Now what is it that causes such failure? Just as the flesh gives you strength to do righteously so it also gives you the power to sin. Whether good acts or evil, all are but the expressions of the same flesh. If the flesh is not furnished opportunity to sin, it is willing to do good; and if once the opportunity to perform good is provided, the flesh will soon revert to sin.

THE BELIEVER'S ULTIMATE ATTITUDE TOWARDS THE FLESH

Make no provision for the flesh.

Romans 13.14b

GOD'S VIEW OF THE FLESH

We Christians need to be reminded once again of God's judgment upon the flesh. "The flesh," says the Lord Jesus, "is of no avail" (John 6.63). Whether it be the sin of the flesh or the righteousness of the flesh, it is futile. That which is born of the flesh, whatever it may be, is flesh, and can never be "unfleshed." Whether it be the flesh in the pulpit, the flesh in the audience, the flesh in prayers, the flesh in consecration, the flesh in reading the Bible, the flesh in singing hymns, or the flesh in doing good—none of these, asserts God, can avail. However much believers may lust in the flesh, God declares it all to be unprofitable; for neither does the flesh profit the spiritual life nor can it fulfill the righteousness of God. Let us now note a few observations concerning the flesh which the Lord through the Apostle Paul makes in the letter to the Romans.

(1) "To set the mind on the flesh is death" (8.6). According to God's view there is spiritual death in the flesh. The only escape is to commit the flesh to the cross. Regardless how competent it is to do good or to plan and plot so as to draw down the approval of men, God has pronounced upon the flesh simply one judgment: death.

(2) "The mind that is set on the flesh is hostile to God" (8.7). The flesh is opposed to God. Not the slightest chance is there of peaceful co-existence. This holds true in regard not only to the sins which issue from the flesh but also to its noblest thoughts and actions. Obviously defiling sins are

hostile to God, but let us observe that righteous acts can be done independently of God as well.

(3) "It does not submit to God's law, indeed it cannot" (8.7). The better the flesh works the farther away it is from God. How many of the "good" people are willing to believe in the Lord Jesus? Their self-righteousness is not righteousness at all; it is actually unrighteousness. None can ever obey all the teaching of the Holy Bible. Whether a person is good or bad, one thing is certain: he does not submit to God's law. In being bad he transgresses the law; in being good he establishes another righteousness outside of Christ and thus misses the purpose of the law ("through the law comes knowledge of sin" 3.20).

(4) "Those who are in the flesh cannot please God" (8.8). This is the final verdict. Regardless how good a man may be, if the doing is out from himself it cannot please God. God is pleased with His Son alone; aside from Him and His work no man nor work can delight God. What is performed by the flesh may seem to be quite good; nevertheless, because it derives from self and is done in natural strength it cannot satisfy God. Man may devise many ways to do good, to improve, and to advance, but these are carnal and cannot please Him. This is not only true of the unregenerate; it is likewise true of the regenerated person. However commendable and effective should anything be that is done in his own strength the believer fails to draw down upon himself the approval of God. God's pleasure or displeasure is not founded upon the principle of good and evil. Rather, God traces the source of all things. An action may be quite correct, yet God inquires, what is its origin?

THE CROSS AND THE DEEPER WORK OF THE HOLY SPIRIT

Because the flesh is grossly deceitful, the believer requires the cross and the Holy Spirit. Once having discerned how his flesh stands before God, he must experience each moment the deeper work of the cross through the Holy Spirit. Just as a Christian must be delivered from the sin of the flesh through the cross, so he must now be delivered from the righteousness of the flesh by the same cross. And just as by walking in the Holy Spirit the Christian will not follow the flesh unto sin, so too by walking in the Holy Spirit he will not follow the flesh unto self-righteousness.

As a fact outside the believer the cross has been accomplished perfectly and entirely: to deepen it is not possible. As a process within the believer the cross is experienced in an ever deepening way: the Holy Spirit will teach and apply the principle of the cross in point after point. If one is faithful and obedient he will be led into continually deeper experiences of what the cross has indeed accomplished for him. The cross objectively is a finished absolute fact to which nothing can be added; but subjectively it is an unending progressive experience that can be realized in an ever more penetrating way.

We must understand that within man two different life principles exist. Many of us live a mixed life, obeying one and then the other of these two different principles. Sometimes we entirely depend on the Spirit's energy; at other times we mix in our own strength. Nothing seems to be stable and steadfast. "Do I make my plans like a worldly man, ready to say Yes and No at once?" (2 Corinthians 1.17). A characteristic of the flesh is its fickleness: it alternates between Yes and No and vice versa. But the will of God is: "Walk not according to the flesh (not even for a moment) but according to the Spirit" (Romans 8.4). We ought to accept God's will.

"In him also you were circumcised with a circumcision made without hands, by putting off the body of flesh in the circumcision of Christ" (Colossians 2.11). We should be willing to allow the cross, like a knife in circumcision, to cut off completely everything which pertains to the flesh. Such incision must be deep and clean so that nothing of the flesh is left concealed or can remain. The cross and the curse are inextricable (inseparable) (Galatians 3.13). When we consign our flesh to the cross we hand it over to the curse, acknowledging that in the flesh abides no good thing and that it deserves nothing but the curse of God. Without this heart attitude it is exceedingly difficult for us to accept the circumcision of the flesh. Every affection, desire, thought, knowledge, intent, worship and work of the flesh must go to the cross.

DELIVERANCE FROM SIN AND THE SOUL LIFE

Knowing this, that our old man has been crucified with Him, that the body of sin might be annulled, that we should no longer serve sin.

Romans 6.6 (Darby)

Romans 6 lays the foundation for the Christian's deliverance from sin. Such deliverance God provides for every believer; all may enter in. Moreover, let us be unmistakably clear that this liberation from the power of sin may be experienced the very hour a sinner accepts the Lord Jesus as Savior and is born anew. He need not be a long-time believer and undergo numerous defeats before he can receive this gospel. Delay in accepting the gospel according to Romans 6 is due either to the incomplete gospel he has heard or to his unwillingness in wholly accepting and fully yielding to it. Whereas actually this blessing should be the common possession of all the newly born.

Chapter 6 begins with a call to reminisce, not to anticipate. It directs our attention to the past, to what is already ours: "Knowing this, that our old man has been crucified with him, that the body of sin might be annulled, that we should no longer serve sin" (v.6 Darby). In this single verse we find three major elements—

     (1) "sin" (singular in number) ;
     (2) "old man"; and
     (3) "body" (the body of sin).

These three are vastly different in nature and play unique roles in the act of sinning. Sin here is that which commonly is called the *root* of sin. The Bible informs us that we were formerly slaves of sin. Sin had been the master. First of all therefore, we need to recognize that sin possesses power, for it enslaves us. It emits this power incessantly to draw us into obedience to its old man so that we might sin. The old man represents the sum total of everything we inherit from Adam. We can recognize the old man by knowing what the new man is, because whatever is not of the new man must belong to the old. Our new man embraces everything which flows newly from the Lord at our regeneration. Hence the old man betokens everything in our personality which is outside the new—our old personality and all which belongs to the old nature. We sin because this old man loves sin and is under its power. Now the body of sin refers to this body of ours. This corporeal (bodily) part of man has become the inevitable puppet in all our sinning. It is labeled the body of sin because it likewise is subject to the power of sin, fully laden with the lusts and desires of sin. And it is through this body that sin manages to express itself, else it will be merely an invisible power.

Now how can a man be delivered from sin? Some theorize that since sin is the first cause we must annihilate it in order to attain victory; accordingly they advocate "the eradication of sin." Once the root of sin is pulled out, think these, we never shall sin again and are obviously sanctified. Others argue that we must subdue our body if we desire to overcome sin, for is it not our body, they ask, which practices sin? So there arises in Christendom a group of people who promote asceticism. They use many techniques to suppress themselves for they anticipate that once they overcome the demands of their bodies they shall be holy. None of these is God's way. Romans 6.6 is transparent as to His way. He neither eradicates the root of sin within nor suppresses the body without. Rather, God deals with the old man in between.

The Lord Jesus in going to the cross took with Him not only our sins but also our beings. Paul enunciates this fact by proclaiming "that our old man has been crucified with him." The verb "crucified" in the original is in the aorist tense, connoting that our old man was once and forever crucified with Him. As the cross of Christ is a fact accomplished, so our being crucified with Him is additionally an accomplished fact. Who ever questions the reality of the crucifixion of Christ? Why, then, should we doubt the reality of the crucifixion of our old man?

Many saints, upon hearing the truth of co-death, immediately assume that they ought to die, and so they try their best to crucify themselves. Either lack of God's revelation or lack of faith accounts for this attitude. They not only do this themselves; they teach others so to do as well. The results are too obvious: no power is theirs to be freed from sin and their old man they feel will not die.

This is a grievous misjudgment. The Bible never instructs us to crucify ourselves. Precisely the opposite are we told! We are taught that when Christ went to Calvary He took us there and had us crucified. We are not instructed to begin crucifying ourselves now; instead the Scriptures assure us that our old man was dealt with at the time Christ went to the cross. Romans 6.6 alone is sufficient to substantiate this. There is not the remotest idea conveyed of desiring to crucify ourselves, nor does the Word in the slightest sense imply that our crucifixion awaits realization. The verse in Romans 6 permits no room for doubt when it categorically pronounces that we were crucified with Christ, a fact already accomplished. This is truly the effect of the most precious phrase in the Bible—in Christ." It is because we are in Him and are united with Him that we can say that when Christ went to the cross we went there in Him, that when Christ was crucified we too were crucified in Him. What a wonderful reality that we are in Christ!

What is the consequence of the crucifixion of our old man? Again the answer comes to us unequivocally—"that the body of sin might be annulled." "Annulled" should be rendered "withered" or "unemployed." Beforehand when sin stirred, our old man responded and consequently the body practiced sin. With the crucifixion of the old man and its replacement by the new man, sin may still stir within and attempt to exert its pressure, but it fails to find the consent of the old man in driving the body to sin. Sin can no longer tempt the believer for he is a new man; the old has died. The body's occupation was formerly that of sinning, but this body of sin is now disemployed because the old man was set aside. It is not able to sin and hence has been denied its job. Praise the Lord, this is what He has furnished us.

Why does God crucify our old man with Christ and render our body jobless? His purpose is that "we should no longer serve sin." What God has done in this regard makes it possible for us not to yield thereafter to the pressure of sin nor to be bound by its power. Sin will exercise no dominion over us. Hallelujah! We must praise God for this deliverance.

How shall we enter into such blessing? Two elements are indispensable. First, "reckon yourselves dead to sin and alive to God in Christ Jesus" (Romans 6.11 Darby). This is the essential of faith. When God avows that our old man was crucified with Christ we believe His Word and "reckon ourselves as dead." How then do we die? "We reckon ourselves as dead to sin." When God affirms that we are resurrected with Christ we again trust His Word and "reckon ourselves alive." How then do we live? "We reckon ourselves as alive to God." This reckoning is none other than believing God according to His Word. When God says our old man was crucified, we account ourselves dead; when He insists we are made alive, we reckon ourselves as alive. The failure of many lies in the desire to feel, to see and to experience this crucifixion and resurrection before trusting in the Word of God. These do not realize God has done it already in Christ and that if only, they would believe His Word by reckoning that what He has done is true, His Holy Spirit would give them the experience. His Spirit would communicate to them what is in Christ.

Second, "neither yield your members instruments of unrighteousness to sin, but yield yourselves to God as alive from among the dead and your members instruments of righteousness to God" (Romans 6.13 Darby). This is the essential of consecration. If we persist in holding on to something which God wants us to relinquish, sin shall have dominion over us, and our reckoning shall be futile. If we fail to yield our members as godly instruments of righteousness to speak and do what He desires and go where He directs, should we be surprised we are not yet delivered from sin? Whenever we refuse to relinquish or we offer resistance to God, sin shall return to its dominion. Under such circumstances we naturally lose the power to reckon, that is, to believe God's Word. In our ceasing to exercise faith and to reckon, can we still be said to be positionally in Christ? Yes, but we are living no longer in Him according to the sense of the "abide in Me" of John 15. Accordingly we are unqualified to experience what is factual in Christ, even our crucifixion.

THE SOUL AS LIFE

When we say the soul is the natural life of man we mean it is the power which preserves us alive in the flesh. Our soul *is* our life. The original word employed in Genesis 1.21, 24 for "living creature(s)" is "soul" because this soul is the life human beings and other living creatures share in common. This is the power we naturally possess and by which we live before our regeneration; it is the life which every man has. The Greek lexicon gives the original meaning of *psuche* as "animal life"; so that soul life is what makes man a living creature. It belongs to the natural. Though the soul life may not necessarily be evil—since many sins have been overcome by believers through their old man being crucified with Christ—

yet it remains natural. It is the life of man; hence it is most human. It makes man a perfectly human being. Perhaps it is good, loving and humble. Nonetheless it is but human.

This life is entirely distinct from the new life the Holy Spirit gives us at new birth. What the Holy Spirit imparts is God's uncreated life; this other is but man's created life. The Holy Spirit grants us a supernatural power; this other is merely the natural. The Holy Spirit gives the *zoe*; this other is the *psuche*.

Life is that power within a man which animates every member of his body. Hence this inward soulical power finds expression through the outward physical activity. The outer activity is but the effect of the inner power. What therefore lies unseen behind the activity is the substance of life. All we naturally "are" is included in that life. This is our soul life.

When a believer accepts the grace of our Lord Jesus in being his substitute on the cross, although he may remain woefully ignorant of his being crucified with Christ he is given God's life nonetheless and has his spirit quickened. This imparted new life brings with it a new nature as well. Hence there now exists both two lives and two natures in the believer: the soul life and the spirit life on the one side, the sin nature and God's nature on the other.

These two natures—old and new, sinful and godly—are fundamentally unalike, irreconcilable and unmixable. The new and the old daily strive for authority over the whole man. During this initial stage the Christian is a babe in Christ because he is yet fleshly. Most variable and most painful are his experiences, punctuated by both successes and failures. Later on he comes to know the deliverance of the cross and learns how to exercise faith in reckoning the old man as crucified with Christ. He is thereby freed from that sin which has paralyzed the body. With his old man crucified the believer is empowered to overcome and enjoys in actual experience the promise that "sin will have no dominion over you."

With sin under his feet and all lusts and passions of the flesh behind his back, the believer now enters a new realm. He may picture himself wholly spiritual. When he turns to eye those others who remain entangled in sin he cannot but feel elated and wonder how he has reached the summit of spiritual life. Little does this one realize that far from being completely spiritual he still remains partially carnal; he is yet a soulish or carnal Christian.

THE EXPERIENCE OF SOULISH BELIEVERS

For I know that nothing good dwells in me, that is, in my flesh: for the willing is present in me, but the doing of the good is not.

Romans 7.18 (NASV)

The soul varies inevitably from person to person. It cannot be stereotyped. Each of us has his particular individuality—a uniqueness which will extend on into eternity. It is not destroyed at our regeneration. Otherwise, in the eternity to come life will be most colorless indeed! Now since there is this variation in the *souls* of all men, it naturally follows that the life of *soulish* believers will likewise vary from person to person. Consequently, we can speak here only in general terms and shall merely present the more prominent features, against which God's children may then compare their experiences.

Soulish believers are inordinately curious. For example, simply for the sake of knowing what the future holds do they try to satisfy their curiosity by studying thoroughly the prophecies of the Bible.

Carnal Christians tend to show off their differences and superiorities in clothing, speech or deeds. They desire to shock people into a recognition of all their undertakings. Of course, such a tendency may have been theirs before conversion; but they find it hard ever afterwards to overcome this natural propensity.

Unlike spiritual Christians, who seek not so much the explanation as the experience of being one with God, these believers look diligently for an understanding in their mind. They like to argue and to reason. Failure of their life experience to catch up with their ideal is not what worries them; it is their inability to *understand* this lack of spiritual experience which troubles them! They conjecture that knowing mentally is possessing experientially. This is a tremendous deception.

Most soulish believers assume an attitude of self-righteousness, though often it is scarcely detectable. They hold tenaciously to their minute opinions. It is doubtless correct to hold fast the basic and essential doctrines of the Bible, but certainly we can afford to grant others latitude on minor points. We may have the conviction that what we believe is absolutely right, yet for us to swallow a camel but also to strain out a gnat is not at all pleasing to the Lord. We ought to lay aside the small differences and pursue the common objective.

Carnal believers are moved easily. On one occasion they may be extremely excited and happy, on another occasion, very despondent and sad. In the happy moment they judge the world too small to contain them, and so they soar on wings to the heavens; but in the moment of sadness they conclude that the world has had enough of them and will be glad to be rid of them. There are times of excitement when their hearts are stirred as though a fire were burning within or a treasure had suddenly been found. Equally are there times of depression when the heart is not so stirred but rather gives way to a feeling of loss, making them most dejected. Their joy and their sorrow alike turn largely upon feeling. Their lives are susceptible to constant changes for they are governed by their emotions.

Over-sensitivity is another trait which generally marks the soulish. Very difficult are they to live with because they interpret every move around them as aimed at them. When neglected they become angry. When they suspect changing attitudes towards them, they are hurt. They easily become intimate with people, for they literally thrive on such affection. They exhibit the sentiment of inseparability. A slight change in such a relationship will give their soul unutterable pains. And thus these people are deceived into thinking they are suffering for the Lord.

Oftentimes a carnal Christian is troubled by outside matters. Persons or affairs or things in the world around readily invade his inward man and disturb the peace in his spirit. Place a soulish one in a joyful surrounding and joyful he will be. Put him in a sorrowful environment and sorrowful will he be. He lacks creative power. Instead, he takes on the complexion peculiar to that with which or whom he may be associated.

Christians who thrive on the soul life are very proud. This is because they make self the center. However much they may try to give the glory to God and acknowledge any merit as of God's grace, carnal believers have their mind set upon self. Whether accounting their lives good or bad their thoughts revolve around themselves. They have not yet lost themselves in God. These feel greatly hurt if they are laid aside either in work or in the judgment of others. They cannot bear to be misunderstood or criticized because they—unlike their more spiritual brethren—still have not learned to accept gladly God's orderings, whether resulting in uplift or in rejection. Unwilling are they to appear inferior, as being despised. Even after they have received grace to know the actual state of their natural life as most corrupt and even after they may have humbled themselves before God—counting their lives to be the worst in the world, these nevertheless ironically end up regarding themselves more humble than the rest. They boast in their humility! Pride is deeply bred in the bone.

THE WORKS OF SOULISH BELIEVERS

The soulish are second to none in the matter of works. They are most active, zealous and willing. But they do not labor because they have received God's order; they labor instead because they have zeal and capacity so to do. They believe *doing* God's work is good enough, unaware that only doing the labor of God's *appointment* is truly commendable. These individuals have neither the heart to trust nor the time to wait. They never sincerely seek the will of God. On the contrary, they labor according to their ideas, with a mind teeming with schemes and plans. Because they diligently work, these Christians fall into the error of looking upon themselves as far more advanced than their leisurely brethren. Who can deny, however, that with God's grace the latter can easily be more spiritual than the former?

The labor of soulish believers chiefly depends upon feeling. They take to work only when they feel up to it; and if these congenial feelings cease while working they will quit automatically. They can witness to people for hours on end without weariness if they experience within their hearts a burning and unspeakably joyful feeling. But if they sustain a coldness or dryness within they will scarcely speak, or not even speak at all, in the face of the greatest need—as, say, before a death-bed situation. With tingling warmth they can run a thousand miles; without it, they will not move a tiny step. They cannot ignore their feelings to the extent of speaking when stomach is empty to a Samaritan woman or talking while eyes are drowsy to a Nicodemus.

Carnal Christians crave works; yet amid many labors they are unable to maintain calm in their spirit. They cannot fulfill God's orders quietly as can the spiritual believers. Much work disturbs them. Outer confusion causes inner unrest. Their hearts are governed by outward matters. Being "distracted with much serving" (Luke 10.40) is the characteristic of the work of any soulish believer.

Carnal Christians are readily discouraged in their exertions. They lack that quiet confidence which trusts God for His work. Regulated as they are by their internal sensations and external environments, they cannot appreciate the "law of faith." Upon feeling that they have failed, though not necessarily true, they give up. They faint when the surroundings appear dark and uninviting to them. They have not yet entered into the rest of God.

The soulish are experts at finding fault, although they are not necessarily stronger themselves. Quick are the soulish to criticize and slow are they to forgive. When they investigate and correct the shortcomings in others they exude a kind of self-sufficient and superior attitude. Their way in sometimes helping people is correct and legal, but their motivation is not always right.

The soulish love to use spiritual phraseology. They learn by heart a large spiritual vocabulary which they invariably employ whenever convenient. They use it in preaching as well as in praying, but without any heart.

A vaunting ambition marks out those who live in the realm of the soul. The first place is often their desire. They are vainglorious in the Lord's work. They aspire to be powerful workers, greatly used by the Lord. Why? That they may gain a place, obtain some glory. They like to compare themselves with others: probably not so much with those whom they do not know as with those with whom they work. Such contending and striving in the dark can be very intense. Those who are spiritually behind they despise, regarding them as too laggard; those who are spiritually great they downgrade, visualizing themselves as almost equal. Their unceasing pursuit is to be great, to be the head. They hope their work will prosper so that they may be well spoken of. These desires of course are deeply concealed in their hearts, barely detectable by others. Although these longings may indeed be well-nigh hidden and mingled with other and purer motives, the presence of such base desires is nonetheless an irrefutable fact.

Because the carnal are greatly talented—active in thought, rich in emotion—they readily arouse people's interest and stir the latter's hearts. Consequently, soulish Christians usually possess magnetic personalities. They can quickly win the acclamation of the common people. Yet the fact remains that they actually are lacking in spiritual power. They do not contain the living flow of the power of the Holy Spirit. What they have is of their own. People are aware that they possess something, but this something does not impart spiritual vitality to others. They appear to be quite rich; they are really quite poor.

THE DANGERS OF SOULISH LIFE

Put no confidence in the flesh.

Philippians 3.3b (NASV)

Believers who are reluctant to, or who fail to, attain what God has ordained are subject to certain hazards. God's intent is for His children to walk by the spirit, not by the soul or body. Failure to live in the spirit incurs loss. Its dangers are at least threefold.

1. *The danger of the spirit being suppressed.* The perfect and complete order of God's operation is first to move in the human spirit, next to enlighten the mind of the soul, and finally to execute through the body. Such an arrangement is of vital significance.

Many of God's children, however, do not perceive the movement of the Holy Spirit. They cannot distinguish between the spiritual and the soulical. They often construe the soulical to be the spiritual and vice versa, consequently drawing much upon the energy of the soul for their walk and work to the detrimental suppression of the spirit. They assume they are walking according to the spirit while in truth they are walking according to the soul. Such foolishness throttles their spirit from cooperating with God's Spirit and thereby interrupts what He is wishing to do in their lives.

As long as Christians dwell in the soul they move according to the thoughts, imaginations, plans and visions of their mind. They covet joyful sensations and are mastered by their feelings. When they have sensuous experiences they are elated, but when bereft of such experiences they can hardly lift a finger. They are therefore powerless to live in the realm of the spirit. Their feelings become their life, and as their feelings change so do they too. This amounts to nothing more than walking after the sensations of their outward soul and body instead of living out from the center of their being which is the spirit. Their spiritual sensitivity, overpowered by the body and the soul, grows dull. These believers can only sense matters in the soul or in the body; they have lost the spiritual sense. Their spirit is disabled from cooperating with God and their spiritual growth is arrested. They are no longer capable of acquiring power and guidance in their spirit for warfare and worship. If a person denies to his spirit complete ascendancy over his being or fails to draw upon its power to live, he shall never mature.

2. *The danger of retreating into the body realm.* Many fleshly works enumerated in Galatians 5 naturally have their origin in the lusts of the human body, but quite a few others indicate as well the activities of the soul. "Selfishness, dissension, party spirit" distinctly flow from man's self or personality. They are the consequence of the numerous diverse thoughts and opinions held on to among saints. What is important to note here is the fact that these exertions of the soul are listed together with such sins of the body as "immorality, impurity, licentiousness, drunkenness, carousing." This ought to remind us of how closely entwined are the soul and the body. These two in reality are inseparable, because the body we are now in is a "soulical body" (1 Corinthians 15.44 literal). Should a believer therefore merely seek to subdue his sinful nature and not his natural life too, he shall find himself, after a short period of experiencing victory over sin, once again tumbling into the realm of the body of sin. Though he may not return to those uglier forms of sin, nevertheless he remains bound by sin.

3. *The danger of the power of darkness taking advantage.* The Letter of James, written to believers, distinctly delineates the relation between soul life and satanic work:

Who is wise and understanding among you? By his good life let him show his works in the meekness of wisdom. But if you have bitter jealousy and selfish ambition in your hearts, do not boast and be false to the truth. This wisdom is not such as comes down from above, but is earthly, unspiritual (literally soulish), devilish. (3.13-15)

There is a wisdom which comes from Satan and it is the same as that which can arise at times out of the human soul. The "flesh" is the devil's factory; his operation in the soulical part of the flesh is as active as in the bodily part. These verses explain how bitter jealousy springs from the seeking of soulish wisdom. It is through the activity of the devil in the human soul. Christians are aware that the adversary can entice people to sin, but do they equally realize he can inject thoughts into man's mind? The fall of man was due to the love of knowledge and of wisdom. Satan is employing the same tactic today in order to retain the believer's soul as his operative center.

The scheme of Satan is to preserve for himself as much of our old creation as possible. If he fails to entangle believers in sin, he will next try to induce them to keep their natural life by taking advantage of their ignorance of his wiles or their unwillingness to yield to the Spirit. For if he does not succeed, all the armies of hell shall soon be totally disemployed. The more believers unite with the Lord in spirit the more the life of the Holy Spirit shall flow into their spirit and the more the cross shall work in them daily. Hence they shall be delivered increasingly from the old creation and shall yield less ground to Satan from which to operate. Let it be known that all the endeavors of Satan, whether by enticement or by attack, are perpetrated in our old creation. He dare not waste his energy on our "new creation," God's Own life. That is the reason he unceasingly attempts to persuade the children of God to retain something of the old creation—be it sin or the beautiful natural life—so that he may continue to operate. How he conspires against believers and confuses them into loving their self life, despite the fact they have hated sin.

LESSON THIRTEEN

THE CROSS AND THE SOUL

He who does not take his cross and follow me, is not worthy of me. He who finds his (soul) life will lose it, and he who loses his [soul] life for my sake will find it.

Matthew 10.38-39

THE CALL OF THE CROSS

On at least four separate occasions and recorded in the four Gospels the Lord Jesus called His disciples to deny their soul life, deliver it to death, and then to follow Him. The Lord fully recognizes that this is the *sine qua non* for any believer who desires to follow Him and to be perfect like Him in serving men and in obeying God. The Lord Jesus mentions soul life in all these calls, yet He places a different emphasis upon each. Since soul life can express itself in various ways, the Lord stresses a different aspect each time. Anyone who would be a disciple of the Lord must give close attention to what He has said. He is summoning men to commit their natural life to the cross.

THE CROSS AND SOULICAL AFFECTION

"He who does not take his cross and follow me is not worthy of me. He who finds his (soul) life will lose it, and he who loses his (soul) life for my sake will find it" (Matthew 10.38-39).

These verses beckon us to relinquish our soul life and hand it over to the cross for the Lord's sake. The Lord Jesus explains how a man's foes shall be those of his household; how the son, for the sake of the Lord, shall be torn away from his father, the daughter from her mother, the daughter-in-law from her mother-in-law. This constitutes a cross and the cross

64

denotes being crucified. It is our natural inclination to cherish our beloved ones. We are happy to listen to them and willing to respond to their bidding. But the Lord Jesus calls us to not rebel against God because of our beloved ones. When the desire of God and the desire of man are in conflict, we must for the Lord's sake take up our cross by committing our soulical affection to death, even though the person we love is dear to us, and even though under ordinary circumstances we would be most reluctant to hurt him. The Lord Jesus beckons us in this way so that we may be purified from our natural love. It is for this reason that He therefore declares that the one "who loves father or mother more than me is not worthy of me; and he who loves son or daughter more than me is not worthy of me" (v.37).

"If anyone comes to me and does not hate his own father and mother and wife and children and brothers and sisters, yes, and even his own life, he cannot be my disciple. Whoever does not bear his own cross and come after me, cannot be my disciple" (Luke 14.26-27). Now Matthew shows us in the matter of affection how believers ought to choose loving the Lord first rather than one's family; while Luke signifies what attitude must be maintained towards the love which arises from our soul life—we ought to hate it. Strictly speaking, we are not to love just because the objects of our affection are those whom we would naturally love. Dear and near as parents, brothers, sisters, wives and children are to us, they are listed among the forbidden. Such human love flows from soul life which will cling to its heart desires and will call for love in return. The Lord maintains that such soul life needs to be delivered to death. Though we do not now see Him, He wants us to love Him. He desires us to deny our natural love. He wishes to rid us of our natural love towards others so that we will not love with our own love. Of course He wills that we should love others, but not with our natural soulical affection.

If we love, let it be for the sake of the Lord and not for their sake. A new relationship comes to us in the Lord. We should receive from Him His love so that we may love others. In a word, our love must be governed by the Lord. Should He desire us to, we must love even our enemies: if He does not ask us to, we cannot love even the dearest of our household. He does not want our heart to be attached anywhere because He wants us to serve Him freely.

This new love relationship being the case, the soul life must be denied. That is a cross. In so obeying Christ as to disregard his natural affection, a believer's natural love suffers intensely. Such sorrow and pain becomes a practical cross to him. Deep are the heart wounds and many are the tears when one has to forfeit the one he loves. These inflict intense sufferings upon our lives. How very loathe the soul is to yield up its beloved for the Lord's sake! But through this very action is the soul delivered to death; yea, it even becomes willing to die; and thus the believer is liberated from the power of the soul. Upon losing its natural affection on the cross the soul cedes ground to the Holy Spirit that He may shed abroad in the believer's heart the love of God, and enable him to love in God and with the love of God.

THE CROSS AND SELF

"Then Jesus told his disciples, 'If any man would come after me, let him deny himself and take up his cross and follow me. For whoever would save his life will lose it, and whoever loses his life for my sake will find it'" (Matthew 16.24-25). Again our Lord is calling His disciples to take up the cross by presenting their soul life to death. Whereas the emphasis in Matthew 10 is the affection of the soul, here in Matthew 16 the self of the soul is brought into view. From the preceding verses we learn that the Lord Jesus was at that time unfolding to His disciples His approaching rendezvous with the cross. Out of his intense love for the Lord Peter blurted out: "Lord, pity

Yourself." Peter was mindful of man, urging his Master to spare Himself from the pains of the cross in the flesh. Peter failed to understand how man ought to be mindful of the things of God, even in such a matter as death on a cross. He failed to see that concern for God's will must far exceed the concern for self. His attitude went something like this: "Though by dying on the cross one shall obey God's will and fulfill God's purpose, yet ought not one to think of himself? Should he not be mindful of the pain he will have to bear? Lord, pity Yourself!"

What was the Lord's answer to Peter? He sternly rebuked him and declared that such an idea as self-pity could only have originated from Satan. Then he continued by saying to His disciples: "It is not I alone who will go to the cross, but all you who follow and desire to be disciples must also go there. As my way is, so shall your way be. Do not incorrectly imagine that I alone must do God's will; all of you as well shall do His will. In the same manner as I am not mindful of myself and unconditionally obey God's will even to the death of the cross, so shall you deny your self life and be willing to lose it in obedience to God." Peter told the Lord: "You must *pity Yourself!*" The Lord came back with: "You must *deny yourself.*"

There is a price to pay in following God's will. The flesh trembles at such a prospect. While soul life reigns supreme within us we are unfit to accept God's orders because it wishes to follow its will and not God's. When He calls us to deny ourselves through the cross and renounce all for His sake, our natural life instinctively responds with self-pity. This renders us unwilling to pay any cost for God. Hence whenever we choose the narrow way of the cross and endure for Christ's sake, our soul life shall suffer loss. This is how we lose that life. Only in this way can the spiritual life of Christ be enthroned pure and supreme, undertaking within us whatever is well-pleasing to God and beneficial to men.

THE CROSS AND THE SOUL'S LOVE OF THE WORLD

Once again our Lord speaks: "Remember Lot's wife. Whoever seeks to gain his life will lose it, but whoever loses his life will preserve it" (Luke 17.32-33). Although these are by now familiar words to the reader, we must note the Lord here lays stress upon self-denial in relation to the things of this world. How irksome it seems for believers to have their hearts detached from earthly possessions. We need to follow our Lord's admonition to remember Lot's wife, for she was one who did not forget her possessions even in a time of the greatest peril. She was not guilty of having retraced a single step towards Sodom. All she did was look back. But how revealing was that backward glance! Does it not speak volumes concerning the condition of her heart?

It is possible for a believer outwardly to forsake the world and leave everything behind and yet inwardly cling to those very elements he had forsaken for the Lord's sake. It does not require a consecrated person to return to the world or to repossess what he had forsaken in the world to indicate that the soul life is still active. If he but casts one longing glance it is sufficient to disclose to us that he does not truly recognize where the world stands in relation to the cross.

THE CROSS AND SOUL POWER

In the Gospel of John the Lord Jesus touches upon soul life once more. "Truly, truly, I say to you, unless a grain of wheat falls into the earth and dies, it remains alone; but if it dies, it bears much fruit. He who loves his life loses it, and he who hates his life in this world will keep it for eternal life" (12.24-25). He subsequently gives the explanation with these words: "And I, when I am lifted up from the earth, will draw all men to myself" (v.32). John 12 records the most prosperous moment in our Lord's life. Lazarus had been raised from the dead and many Jews believed in Him. Triumphantly He entered into Jerusalem and was acclaimed by the populace. Even Gentiles sought to see Him. From the human viewpoint Calvary would now seem to be quite unnecessary, for could He not easily attract all men to Himself without going to the cross? But He knew better. Although his work appeared to be prosperous, He realized He could not grant life to men without His going to death. Calvary was the only way of salvation. If He died, He would draw all men to Himself and could indeed give life to all.

In John 12 the Lord explicitly describes the operation of the cross. He compares Himself to a grain of wheat. If it does not fall into the earth and die it remains *alone*. But if He be crucified and die, He shall impart life to many. The one condition is death. No death, no fruit. No other way is there to bear fruit than through death.

Our purpose, however, is not simply to learn about the Lord Jesus. We wish beyond this to draw particular attention to its relationship to *our* soul life. The Lord applies the grain of wheat to Himself in verse 24, but in verse 25 He implies that every one of His disciples must follow in His footsteps. He pictures the grain as representing their self life. Just as a grain is unable to bear fruit unless it dies, so there can be no spiritual fruit until the natural life has been broken through death. Here he emphasizes the matter of fruitfulness. While the soul life does possess tremendous power it nevertheless cannot fulfill the work of fruit-bearing. All the energies generated in the soul including talent, gift, knowledge and wisdom, cannot enable believers to bear spiritual fruit. If the Lord Jesus must die to bear fruit so also must His disciples die in order to produce fruit. The Lord regards soulish power as of no help to God in His work of fruit-bearing.

The greatest peril for us in Christian service is to lean upon our selves and to draw upon our soul power—upon our talent, gift, knowledge, magnetism, eloquence or cleverness. The experience of countless spiritual believers confirms that unless our soulishness is definitely delivered to death and its life at all times inhibited from operating, it will be most active in service. If this is true of them, then how can those who are unwilling to yield up, or unwatchful in denying, their soul life prevent the intrusion of that life? Everything pertaining to our natural life must be handed over to death so that in no sense may we depend upon any of it but be willing instead to be led through death's darkness of no support, no sensation, no sight, no understanding, and silently trust God Himself to work until we emerge on the other side of resurrection to possess a more glorious life. "He who hates his life in this world will keep it for eternal life." Our soul is not annihilated; rather, by passing through death it affords God an opportunity to communicate His life to us. Not to lose the soul life in death shall mean great loss for the believer; but in losing it he will save it for eternity.

LESSON FOURTEEN

SPIRITUAL BELIEVERS AND THE SOUL

The word of God is living and active, sharper than any two-edged sword, piercing to the division of soul and spirit, of joints and marrow, and discerning the thoughts and intentions of the heart.

Hebrews 4.12

Our natural life is a formidable obstacle to spiritual life. Never satisfied with God alone, it invariably adds something extra to God. Hence it is never at peace. Before the self is touched God's children live by very changeable stimulations and sensations. That is why they exhibit a wavy up-and-down existence. Because they allow their soulical energies to mix in with spiritual experiences their ways are often unstable. They accordingly are not qualified to lead others. Their unrelinquished soul power continually deflects them from letting the spirit be central. In the excitement of soulical emotion the spirit suffers great loss in freedom and sensation. Joy and sorrow may imperil the believer's self-control and set self-consciousness on a rampage. The mind, if overly active, may affect and disturb the quietness of the spirit. To admire spiritual knowledge is good, but should it exceed spiritual bounds the result shall be merely letter, not spirit. This explains why many workers, though they preach the most excellent truth, are so cold and dead. Many saints who seek a spiritual walk share a common experience—one of groanings because their soul and spirit are not at one. The thought, will and emotion of their soul often rebel against the spirit, refuse to be directed by the spirit and resort to independent actions which contradict the spirit. The life in their spirit is bound to suffer in such a situation.

Now given a condition like this in the believer, the teaching in Hebrews 4.12 takes on paramount significance. For the

Holy Spirit instructs us therein how to divide spirit and soul experientially. The dividing of these two is not a mere doctrine; it is pre-eminently a life, a must in the believer's walk. Just what is its essential meaning? It means, first of all, that by His Word and through His indwelling Spirit God enables the Christian to differentiate in experience the operations and expressions of the spirit as distinct from those of the soul. Thus he may perceive what is of the spirit and what is of the soul.

The dividing of these two elements denotes additionally that through willing cooperation the child of God can follow a pure spiritual path unimpeded by the soul. The Holy Spirit in Hebrews 4 sets forth the high-priestly ministry of the Lord Jesus and also explains its relationship to us. Verse 12 declares that "the word of God is living and active, sharper than any two-edged sword, piercing to the division of soul and spirit, of joints and marrow, and discerning the thoughts and intentions of the heart." And verse 13 follows by informing us that "before him no creature is hidden, but all are open and laid bare to the eyes of him with whom we have to do." These therefore tell us how much the Lord Jesus fulfills His work as High Priest with respect to our spirit and soul. The Holy Spirit compares the believer to a sacrifice on the altar. During the Old Testament period when people presented an offering, they bound their sacrifice to the altar. The priest then came and killed it with a sharp knife, parting it into two and piercing to the division of the joints and marrow, thus exposing to view all that formerly had been hidden from human sight. Afterwards it was burned with fire as an offering to God. The Holy Spirit uses this event to illustrate the work of the Lord Jesus towards believers and the experience of the believers in the Lord. Just as the sacrifice of old was cut asunder by the priests' knife so that the joints and marrow were exposed and divided, even so the believer today has his soul and spirit split apart by the Word of God as used by our High Priest, the Lord Jesus. This is that the soul may no longer affect the spirit nor the spirit any more be under the soul's authority; rather, each will find its rightful place, with neither confusion nor mixture.

As the priest of old split the sacrifice, so our High Priest today divides our soul and spirit. As the priestly knife was of such sharpness that the sacrifice was cut into two, piercing to the separation of the closely knit joints and marrow, so the Word of God which the Lord Jesus currently uses is keener than any two-edged sword and is able to split cleanly apart the most intimately related spirit and soul there may be.

The Word of God is "living" for it has living power: "active" because it knows how to work: "sharper than any two edged sword" since it can pierce into the spirit. What God's Word has penetrated is much deeper than the soul; it reaches into the innermost spirit. God's Word leads His people into a realm more profound than one of mere sensation; it brings them into the realm of the eternal spirit. Those who wish to be established in God must know the meaning of this penetration into the spirit. The Holy Spirit alone can teach us what is soul life and what is spirit life. Only after we learn how to differentiate experientially these two kinds of life and come to apprehend their respective values, are we delivered from a shallow, loose, sensational walk into that which is deep, firm and spiritual. Only then do we come into rest. The soul life can never furnish us rest. But please note that this must be known *in experience*; simply understanding in the mind will merely make us more soulish.

We need to pay special attention to this piercing and dividing. The Word of God plunges into the soul as well as into the spirit in order to effect the division of these two. The Lord Jesus in His crucifixion had His hands and feet and side pierced. Are we willing to let the cross work in our soul and spirit? A sword pierced through Mary's soul (Luke 2.35). Although her "Son" was given by God, she was required to let go of Him and to relinquish all her authority and demands upon Him. Even though her soul craved to cling tenaciously to Him, Mary must deny her natural affection.

The cleaving of soul and spirit means not only their separation but also a cracking open of the soul itself. Since the spirit is enveloped in the soul, it cannot be reached by the Word of life save through a cracked shell. The Word of the cross plunges in and splits open a way into and through the soul so that God's life can reach the spirit within and liberate it from the bondage of its soulish shell. Having received the mark of the cross, the soul now can assume its proper position of subjection to the spirit. But if the soul fails to become a "thoroughfare" to the spirit, then the former surely will become the latter's chain. These two never agree on any matter. Before the spirit achieves its rightful place of pre-eminence it is challenged persistently by the soul. While the spirit is striving to gain freedom and mastery the strong soul power exerts its utmost strength to suppress the spirit. Only after the cross has done its work on the soulish life is the spirit liberated. If we remain ignorant of the damage this discord between the spirit and soul can bring or remain unwilling to forsake the pleasure of a sensuous walk, we shall make hardly any spiritual progress. As long as the siege thrown up by the soul is not lifted the spirit cannot be freed.

Upon carefully studying the teaching of this fragment of Scripture, we may conclude that the dividing of spirit and soul hinges upon two factors: the cross and God's Word. Before the priest could use his knife the sacrifice had to be placed on the altar. The altar in the Old Testament speaks of the cross in the New Testament. Believers cannot expect their High Priest to wield God's sharp Sword, His Word which pierces to the separation of soul and spirit, unless first they are willing to come to the cross and accept its death. Lying on the altar always precedes the plunging of the sword. Hence all who desire to experience the parting of soul and spirit must answer the Lord's call to Calvary and lay themselves unreservedly on the altar, trusting their High Priest to operate with His keen Sword to the dividing asunder of their spirit and soul. For us to lie on the altar is our free-will offering well-pleasing to God; to use the sword to divide is the work of the priest. We should fulfill our part with all faithfulness, and commit the rest to our merciful and faithful High Priest. And at the appropriate time He shall lead us into a complete spiritual experience.

This brings us to the other, and equally significant, aspect of the dividing of spirit and soul. Insofar as the soul's influence and control of the spirit is concerned, the work of the cross is to effect the division of the two; but insofar as the spirit's filling and reigning is concerned, the cross works towards the surrender of the soul's independence so that it may be reconciled completely to the spirit. Believers should seek to experience oneness of spirit and soul. Were we to allow the cross and the Holy Spirit to operate thoroughly in us we would discover that what the soul has relinquished is scarcely a fraction of what it ultimately gains: the dead has now come into fruition, the lost is now kept for eternal life. When our soul is brought under the reins of the spirit it undergoes an immense change. Beforehand it seems to be useless and lost to God because it is employed for self and often moves independently; afterwards God gains our soul, though to man it may appear to be crushed. We become as "those who have faith and keep their souls" (Hebrews 10.39). This is much more profound than what we commonly term "saved," because it points especially to life. Since we have learned not to walk by sensation and sight, we are now able to save our life by faith into serving and glorifying God. "Receive with meekness the implanted word, which is able to save your souls" (James 1.21). As God's Word is implanted we receive its new nature into us and are thus enabled to bear fruit. We obtain the life of the Word from the Word of life. Although the organs of the

75

soul still remain, these organs no longer function through its power; rather, they operate by the power of God's Word. This is "the salvation of your souls" (1 Peter 1.9).

THE HOLY SPIRIT AND THE BELIEVER'S SPIRIT

It is the Spirit himself bearing witness with our spirit that we are children of God.

Romans 8.16

THE REGENERATION OF MAN

Why must a sinner be born anew? Why must he be born from above? Why must there be a regeneration of the spirit? Because man is a fallen spirit. A fallen spirit needs to be reborn that it may become a new one. Just as Satan is a fallen spirit, so is man; only he has a body. Satan's fall came before man's; we therefore can learn about our fallen state from Satan's plunge. Satan was created as a spirit that he might have direct communion with God. But he fell away and became the head of the powers of darkness. He now is separated from God and from every godly virtue. This, however, does not signify that Satan is non-existent. His fall only took away his right relationship with God. Similarly, man in his fall also sank into darkness and separation from God. Man's spirit still exists but is separated from God, powerless to commune with Him and incapable of ruling. Spiritually speaking, man's spirit is dead. Nonetheless, as the spirit of the sinful archangel exists forever so the spirit of sinful man continues too. Because he has a body his fall rendered him a man of the flesh (Genesis 6.3). No religion of this world, no ethics, culture or law can improve this fallen human spirit. Man has degenerated into a fleshly position; nothing from himself can return him to a spiritual state. Wherefore regeneration or regeneration of the spirit is absolutely necessary. The Son of God alone can restore us to God, for He shed His blood to cleanse our sins and give us a new life.

Immediately the sinner believes in the Lord Jesus he is born anew. God grants him His uncreated life that the sinner's spirit may be made alive. The regeneration of a sinner occurs *in his spirit.* God's work begins without exception within the man, from the center to the circumference. How unlike Satan's pattern of work! He operates from the outer to the inner. God aims first to renew man's darkened spirit by imparting life to it, because it is this spirit which God originally designed to receive His life and to commune with Him. God's intent after that is to work out from the spirit to permeate man's soul and body.

THE HOLY SPIRIT AND REGENERATION

When regenerated, man's spirit is made alive through the incoming of God's life. The Holy Spirit is the prime mover in this task. He convinces the world of sin and of righteousness and of judgment (John 16.8). He prepares human hearts to believe in the Lord Jesus as Savior. The work of the cross has been fulfilled by the Lord Jesus, but it is left to the Holy Spirit to apply this finished work to the sinner's heart. We ought to know the relationship between the cross of Christ and its application by the Spirit. The cross accomplishes all, but the Holy Spirit administers to man what it has accomplished. The cross grants us position; the Holy Spirit gives us experience. The cross brings in the fact of God; the Holy Spirit brings about the demonstration of that fact. The work of the cross creates a position and achieves a salvation by which sinners can be saved; the task of the Holy Spirit is to reveal to sinners what the cross has created and achieved so that they may in fact receive it and be saved. The Holy Spirit never functions independently of the cross: without the cross the Holy Spirit has no proper ground from which to operate: without the Holy Spirit the work of the cross is dead, that is, it produces no effect upon men even though it is already effective before God.

While it is the cross which achieves the whole work of salvation, it is the Holy Spirit Who operates directly upon men for their salvation. Hence the Bible characterizes our regeneration as a work of the Holy Spirit: "that which is born of the Spirit is spirit" (John 3.6). The Lord Jesus explains further on that regenerated man is "every one who is born of the Spirit" (v.8). Believers are born anew because the Holy Spirit brings to bear the work of the cross upon them and communicates God's life to their spirit. He is none other than the Executor of God's life. "We live by the Spirit" (Galatians 5.25). If whatever men know comes through their brain without the Holy Spirit regenerating their spirit, then their knowledge will help them not one whit. If their belief rests in man's wisdom and not in God's power, they are merely excited in their soul. They will not last long, for they are not yet newly born. Regeneration comes just to those who believe in their heart (Romans 10.10).

Besides bestowing life to believers at new birth, the Holy Spirit executes a further work of *abiding* in them. How regrettable for us if we forget this! "A new heart I will give you and a new spirit I will put within you ... and I will put my Spirit within you" (Ezekiel 36.26-27). Note that immediately after the clause "a *new* spirit I will put within you" there follows this one of "I will put *my Spirit* within you." The first statement signifies that believers shall receive a new spirit through the renewal of their deadened spirit by the incoming of life. The second has reference to the indwelling or the abiding of the Holy Spirit in that renewed spirit of theirs. Believers at new birth obtain not only a new spirit but also the Holy Spirit dwelling within. Is it not sad that many fail to understand the newness of their spirit *and* the abiding of the Holy Spirit in their new spirit? Christians need not delay many years following regeneration and then suddenly wake up and seek the Holy Spirit; they have His entire personality *abiding* in them—not just visiting them—at the moment they are saved. The Apostle exhorts us on this wise: "Do not grieve the Holy Spirit of God, in whom you were sealed for the day of redemption" (Ephesians 4.30). The use of the word "grieve" here and not "anger" reveals the Holy Spirit's love. "Grieve" it says and not "cause to depart," for "he dwells with you and will be in you" (John 14.17). While every born-again believer does have the Holy Spirit permanently residing in him, nevertheless the plight of the indwelling Spirit may not be the same in all saints—He may be either grieved or gladdened.

Why is it so important to understand that the Holy Spirit dwells in man's innermost depth, deeper within than his organs of thought, feeling and decision? Because unless the child of God perceives this, invariably he shall seek His guidance in his soul. With understanding he shall be delivered from the deception and error of looking to what is outward. The Holy Spirit lives in the remotest recess of our being; there and only there may we expect His working and obtain His guidance. Our prayers are directed to "our Father who art in *heaven*," but the heavenly Father guides from *within* us. If our Counsellor, our Paraclete, resides in our spirit then His guidance must come from within. How tragically deceived we will be if we seek dreams, visions, voices, and sensations in our outer man rather than seeking Him in our inner man!

"It is the Spirit himself bearing witness with our spirit that we are children of God" (Romans 8.16). Man's spirit is the place where man works together with God. How do we know we have been born anew and are therefore children of God? We know because our inner man has been quickened and the Holy Spirit dwells therein. Our spirit is a regenerated, renewed one, and He Who dwells in, yet is distinct from, this new spirit is the Holy Spirit. And the two of them bear witness together.

A SPIRITUAL MAN

According to the riches of his glory he may grant you to be strengthened with might through his Spirit in the inner man.

Ephesians 3.16

A person whose spirit is regenerated and within whom the Holy Spirit abides can still be fleshly for his spirit may yet be under the oppression of his soul or body. Some very definite actions are required if he is to become spiritual.

Generally speaking we will encounter at least two great perils in our life but are enabled to overcome not only the first but the second of them as well. These two perils with their corresponding triumphs are: that of remaining a perishing sinner or becoming a saved believer and that of continuing as a fleshly believer or developing into a spiritual one. As sinner-turned-believer is demonstrably realizable, so carnal-turned-spiritual is likewise attainable. The God Who can change a sinner into a Christian by giving him His life can equally transform the fleshly Christian into a spiritual one by giving him His life more abundantly. Faith in Christ makes one a regenerated believer; obedience to the Holy Spirit makes him a spiritual believer. Just as the right relationship with Christ generates a Christian, so the proper relationship with the Holy Spirit breeds a spiritual man.

God's children already have the Holy Spirit abiding in them, but they may not recognize Him or obey Him. They need to do so completely. They must realize that this indwelling presence is a Person, One Who teaches, guides, and communicates the reality of Christ to them. Until they are willing to acknowledge the foolishness and dullness of their soul and are ready to be taught, they block the way of this Person. It is necessary for them to let Him regulate everything so as to reveal the truth. Except they know in the depth of their being that God's Holy Spirit is indwelling them and unless with their spirit they wait for His teaching, they will not welcome His operation upon their soul life. Only as they cease to seek anything by themselves and only as they take the position of the teachable shall they be taught by the Spirit truth which they are able to digest. We know He verily abides in us when we understand that our spirit, which is deeper than thought and emotion, is God's Holy of Holies by which we commune with the Holy Spirit and in which we wait for His communication. As we acknowledge Him and respect Him, He manifests His power out from the hidden part of our being by extending His life to our soulical and conscious life.

THE STRENGTHENING OF THE HOLY SPIRIT

In order for man's innermost organ to gain dominion over the soul and the body and thus serve as channel for the life of the Spirit to be transmitted to others, there must be His strengthening. Paul prays for believers "that according to the riches of his glory he may grant you to be strengthened with might through his Spirit in the inner man" (Ephesians 3.16). He so prays because he considers it infinitely important. He asks God to strengthen by His Spirit their "inner man," which is the new man in them after they have trusted in the Lord. Therefore the prayer is that the believer's spirit may be strengthened by God's Spirit.·

The effect of having the spirit filled with God's power is to afford it full sway over the soul and the body. Every thought, desire, sensation and intent is now governed by the spirit. The soul can no longer act independently: it becomes instead the spirit's steward.

WALKING ACCORDING TO THE SPIRIT

Transformation from soulish to spiritual does not guarantee that believers never again will walk according to the flesh. On the contrary, an ever present danger exists of falling back into it. Satan is constantly alert to seize every opportunity to cause them to plunge from their lofty position to a life below par. It is therefore highly necessary for God's children to be watchful at all times and to follow the Spirit so that they may remain spiritual.

"In order that the just requirement of the law might be fulfilled in us, who walk not according to the flesh but according to the Spirit . . . (Now) those who live according to the Spirit set their minds on the things of the Spirit. To set . . . the mind on the Spirit is life and peace" (Romans 8.4-6). To follow the spirit is to walk contrary to the flesh. Not following the spirit is walking by the flesh. Many Christians oscillate between these two: now following the one, now following the other. They ought to walk according to the inner man *alone*, which is, to walk according to the spirit's intuition and not for a moment according to the soul or body. In thus following the spirit they invariably shall "set their minds on the things of the spirit." And the result shall be "life and peace."

To live by the spirit means to walk according to intuition. It is to have all one's life, service, and action in the spirit, ever being governed and empowered by it. This preserves the saint in life and peace. Since he cannot remain in a spiritual state unless he walks according to the spirit, then at the very least the saint must understand its various functions and laws if he is to walk well.

To live after the spirit is the Christian's daily task. He ought to perceive that we can live neither by the noblest of feelings nor by the loftiest of thoughts. We must walk according to the guidance accorded us through our intuition. The Holy Spirit expresses His feeling through our spirit's delicate sense. He does not operate directly on our minds, suddenly inducing us to think of something. All His works are done in our innermost depths. If we desire to know His mind we should conduct ourselves in accordance with the intuition of our spirit. At times, however, we may sense something there without comprehending what it means, what it demands, or what it is communicating. Whenever this happens, we must commit ourselves to prayer, asking that our mind may be given understanding. Once we apprehend the meaning of what we have sensed intuitively, we thereafter should behave accordingly. The mind can instantly be enlightened and made to understand the meaning of intuition; but abrupt thoughts which originate with the mind void of intuition ought not to be followed. Solely intuitive teaching represents the Spirit's thought. Only this should we follow.

Such a walk by the spirit requires *reliance* and *faith*. We have seen before how all good actions of the flesh exhibit an attitude of independence towards God. The very nature of the soul is independency. Should believers act in accordance with their thought, feeling and desire, they have no need to spend time before God, to wait for His guidance. Those who follow "the desires of body and mind" (Ephesians 2.3) need not rely upon God. Except Christians realize how useless, how undependable, and how utterly weak they are in seeking to know the will of God, they shall never cultivate a heart of reliance upon Him. To receive God's guidance in their spirit they must wait upon Him therewith; they must refrain from taking their feeling or thought as a guide. Let us remember that whatever we do or can do without trusting, seeking, and waiting upon God is or will be done in the flesh. With fear and trembling we must rely upon God for guidance in the inner depths. This is the sole way to walk according to the spirit.

To walk in this fashion requires faith of the believer. The opposite of sight and feeling is faith. Now it is the soulish person who gains assurance by grasping the things which can be seen and felt; but the person who follows the spirit lives by faith, not by sight. He will not be troubled by the lack of human assistance, nor will he be moved by human opposition. He can trust God even in utter darkness for he has faith in

God. Because he does not depend upon himself, he can trust the unseen power more than his own visible power.

Our aim is to be a spiritual man but not a spirit. If we recognize this distinction our lives shall never be cut and dried. We today are human beings and shall be so eternally, yet the highest achievement of a human being is to develop into a spiritual man. The angels are spirits; they have neither body nor soul. But we humans possess both. We are to be spiritual men and not spirits. The spiritual man shall continue to retain his soul and body; otherwise, he would be reduced to being a spirit instead of a man. No, what is meant by being a spiritual man is that he is under the control of his spirit which has become the highest organ of his whole person. Let us not be mistaken on this point. A spiritual man retains his soul and body; being spiritual does not annihilate these organs nor their respective functions, because these make man what he is. So although the spiritual man does not live by them, he certainly has not annihilated them either. They instead have been renewed through death and resurrection so that they are perfectly united to the spirit and have become instruments for its expression. Hence the emotion, mind and will remain in a spiritual man but are subject entirely to the guidance of the intuition.

The Apostle Paul has described the authentic condition of a spiritual man in 1 Thessalonians: "May the God of peace himself sanctify you wholly; and may your spirit and soul and body be kept sound and blameless at the coming of our Lord Jesus Christ" (5.23). Hence the portrait of the spiritual man which can be drawn from everything which has been said is as follows:

(1) He has God dwelling in his spirit, sanctifying him totally. Its life inundates his entire person so that his every component lives by the spirit life and functions in the spirit's strength.

(2) He does not live by soul life. His every thought, imagination, feeling, idea, affection, desire and opinion is renewed and purified by the Spirit and has been brought into subjection to his spirit. These no longer operate independently.

(3) He still possesses a body, for he is not a disembodied spirit; yet physical weariness, pain, and demand do not impel the spirit to topple from its ascended position. Every member of the body has become an instrument of righteousness.

To conclude, then, a spiritual man is one who belongs to the spirit: the whole man is governed by the inner man: all the organs of his being are subject completely to it. His spirit is what stamps his life as unique—everything proceeds from his spirit, while he himself renders absolute allegiance to it. No word does he speak nor act does he perform according to himself; rather does he deny his natural power each time in order to draw power from the spirit. In a word, a spiritual man lives by the spirit.

LESSON SEVENTEEN

SPIRITUAL WORK

Not by might not by power, but by My Spirit, says the Lord of hosts.

Zechariah 4.6 (NASV)

All God's children are God's servants. Each of them receives some gift from the Lord: none is excepted (Matthew 25.15). God places them in His church and apportions to each a ministry to fulfill. God's objective is not to make the believer's spirit a reservoir of spiritual life which withers after a little while: if God's life becomes stagnant in him he begins to feel parched. No, spiritual life is for spiritual work; spiritual work expresses spiritual life. The secret of that kind of living lies in the incessant flowing of that life to others.

SPIRITUAL POWER

We must desire to be filled with the Holy Spirit experientially if we desire to have power in witnessing for Christ and in combating Satan. More and more people are in hot pursuit of such experiences today. But the question should be raised as to what lies behind such a quest. How many covet that they may boast? How many desire more glory for their flesh? How many hope people will fall effortlessly under their power? We must discern clearly why we solicit the power of the Holy Spirit. If our motive is neither of God nor one with God, we certainly will not be able to obtain the power. God's Holy Spirit does not fall on man's "flesh"; He descends only on God's newly created spirit within the man. We cannot allow the outward man, that is, the flesh, to persist while petitioning God to immerse our inner man, the spirit, in His Spirit. So long as the flesh continues unscathed the Holy Spirit of God shall never descend upon man's spirit, for man would only grow more fleshly and boastful if power were granted him.

It is often observed that Calvary precedes Pentecost. The Holy Spirit is not willing to dispense power to men and women who have not been dealt with by the cross. The path which leads to the upper room in Jerusalem winds by way of Calvary. Only those who are conformed to the death of the Lord can receive the power of the Lord. The Word of God affirms that "upon man's flesh shall it (holy anointing oil) not be poured" (Exodus 30.32 Darby). God's Holy Oil will not be poured upon the flesh, whether it be exceedingly defiled or highly refined. Where the mark of the cross is lacking, there the oil of the Spirit is absent. Through the death of the Lord Jesus God pronounces His verdict upon all who are in Adam: "all must die." Just as the Heavenly Power did not descend until the Lord Jesus died, even so should the believer not expect that Power if he has yet to know the death of the Lord Jesus in experience. Historically, Pentecost followed Calvary; experientially, being filled with the power of the Holy Spirit follows the bearing of the cross.

In seeking the might of the Holy Spirit we must keep our mind clear and our will alive, thereby guarding ourselves from the enemy's counterfeit. We also must let God purge from our life anything sinful, unrighteous or doubtful, that our total being may be presented to the Lord. We then should "receive the promise of the Spirit through faith" (Galatians 3.14). Rest in God trusting that He will fulfill His Word in due course. Do not, however, forget His promise. Should there be delay, use the opportunity for closer scrutiny of your life beneath His light. Gladly accept any feeling which does come with the power; but if God deems it suitable not to accompany power with feeling, simply believe He has indeed fulfilled His Word.

THE INAUGURATION OF SPIRITUAL WORK

To inaugurate a work is no small matter. Christians should never initiate anything presumptuously on the basis of need, profit, or merit. These may not indicate God's will in the slightest. Perhaps He will raise up others to undertake this task or He may suspend it till some other time. Men may feel regretful, but God knows what is best. Hence need, profit and merit cannot serve as indicators for our work.

The book of Acts is the best aid in approaching our work. We do not find there anyone consecrating himself as a preacher nor anyone deciding to do the Lord's work by making himself a missionary or a pastor. What we do see is the Holy Spirit Himself appointing and sending men out to do the work. God never enlists men to His service: He simply sends whom *He* wants. We do not see anyone choosing himself: it is God who chooses His worker. There is positively no ground for man's flesh. When God selects, not even a Saul of Tarsus can withstand; when God does not select, even a Simon cannot buy it. God is the sole master of His work, for He will not permit any human mixture in it. Never does man come to work, but it is always God Who *sends* out to do his work. Spiritual service consequently must be inaugurated by the Lord Himself calling us. It should not be initiated through the persuasion of preachers, the encouragement of friends, or the bent of our natural temperament. None who are shod with fleshly shoes can stand on the holy ground of God's service. Many failures and much waste and confusion which have resulted are due to men's *coming* to work, instead of being sent out to work.

THE AIM OF SPIRITUAL WORK

Spiritual work aims to give life to man's spirit or to build up the life in the spirit. Our labor will be nil in worth or effectiveness if it is not directed towards the spirit lying in the very depths of man. What a sinner needs is life, not some sublime thought. A believer needs whatever can nourish his spiritual life, not mere Bible knowledge. If all we communicate are excellent sermonic divisions, wonderful parables, transcendent abstractions, clever words, or logical arguments, we are but supplying additional thoughts to people's minds, arousing their emotions once again, or activating their will to make one more decision. With a moribund (dull) spirit do they come and with just as moribund a spirit do they depart despite our heavy labors on their behalf. A sinner needs to have his spirit resurrected, not to be able to argue better, shed profuse tears, or make a firmer resolve. Likewise a believer does not require outward edification, since his real lack is inward life more abundant—how he can grow spiritually. Should we focus our attention on the outward man and neglect the inward man, our work will be utterly vain and superficial. Such work equals no work at all, and perhaps it is even worse than no work, for a lot of precious time is undeniably wasted!

The responsibility of Christians is consequently just this: to present their spirits to God as vessels and to consign to death everything pertaining to themselves. Should they neither block their spirit nor attempt to give to others what they have in and of themselves, God can use His children greatly as channels of life for the salvation of sinners and the upbuilding of the saints. Without that, then whatever the listener receives is but the thought, reason and feeling of the worker; he never accepts the Lord as Savior nor is his dead spirit quickened. Realizing that our aim is to furnish life to man's spirit, we ourselves obviously must be duly prepared. By genuinely relinquishing our soul life and relying entirely on the inner man, we shall see that the words the Lord speaks through our mouths continue to be "spirit and life" (John 6.63).

THE CESSATION OF SPIRITUAL WORK

Spiritual work invariably flows with the current of the Holy Spirit—never reluctantly, never under compulsion, hence without need of fleshly strength. This does not imply of course that there is no opposition from the world or attack from the enemy. It simply means the work is done in the Lord with the consciousness of having His anointing. If God still requires the work, the believer will continue to sense himself flowing in the current, no matter how difficult his situation may be. The Holy Spirit aims at expressing spiritual life. Labor accomplished in Him correspondingly develops life in the spirit. Unfortunately many of God's servants frequently are pressed by environment or other factors into working mechanically.

As soon as the individual is aware of it, he ought to inquire whether such "mechanical work" is desired by the Spirit or whether God would call him away to other service. God's servants should know that a task begun spiritually—that is, in the Spirit—may not necessarily continue that way. Many works are initiated by Him, but after He has no more need of them men often desire to keep them going. To regard as forever spiritual whatever is begun by the Holy Spirit is inevitably to change the spiritual into the fleshly.

A spiritual Christian can no longer enjoy the anointing of the Spirit in a work that has become mechanical. When a task is already given up by God as unnecessary and yet is maintained by the Christian because of the outside organization (with or without form) which surrounds it, then it must be carried on by drawing upon his own resources rather than upon the power of God. Should a saint persist in laboring after the spiritual work is terminated, he must employ his soul power as well as physical power to continue on with it. In true spiritual service one must completely deny his natural talent and gift; only in this way can he produce fruit for God. If not, each effort not led by the Holy Spirit does collapse if not supported by one's brain, talent, or gift.

LESSON EIGHTEEN

PRAYER AND WARFARE

*For the weapons of our warfare are not of the flesh, but
divinely powerful for the destruction of fortresses.*

2 Corinthians 10.4 (NASV)

All prayer ought to be spiritual. Unspiritual prayers are not
genuine and can produce no positive result. What abundant
spiritual success there would be were every prayer offered by
believers on earth in fact spiritual! But sad to say, fleshly
prayers are far too numerous. Self-will found therein deprives
them of spiritual fruitfulness. Nowadays Christians appear to
treat prayer as a means to accomplish *their* aims and ideas. If
they possessed just a little deeper understanding, they would
recognize that prayer is but man uttering to God what is *God's*
will. The flesh, no matter where displayed, must be crucified;
it is not permitted even in prayer. No mixing of man's will in
God's work is possible, for He rejects the best of human
intentions and man's most profitable prospects. God does not
will that He should follow what man has initiated. Other than
following God's direction, we have no right to direct Him. We
have no ability to offer save to obey God's guidance. God will
do no work which originates with man, no matter how much
man may pray. He condemns such praying as fleshly.

All spiritual prayers have their source in God. God makes
known to us what we ought to pray by unfolding to us the need
and by giving that need as a burden in our intuitive spirit. Only
an intuitive burden can constitute our call to pray. Yet how we
have overlooked many delicate registrations in the intuition
through carelessness. Our prayer should never exceed the
burden in our intuition. Prayers which are not initiated or
responded to in the spirit originate instead with the believer
himself. They are therefore of the flesh. So that his prayer may
not be fleshly but may be effectual in the spiritual domain,

the child of God ought to confess his weakness that he does not know how to pray (Romans 8.26), and petition the Holy Spirit to teach him. He next should pray according to His instruction. God gives us utterance to pray just as he gives us utterance to preach. The need for the former equals that of the latter. In acknowledging our total weakness, we then are able to depend on the movement of the Holy Spirit within our spirit for uttering His prayer. How empty that work is which is done by the flesh; how likewise fruitless is that prayer which is offered in the flesh.

Not only should we pray with the spirit; we should "pray with the mind also" (1 Corinthians 14.15). In praying, these two must work together. A believer receives in his spirit what he needs to pray and understands in his mind what he has received. The spirit accepts the burden of prayer while the mind formulates that burden in prayerful words. Only in this way is the prayer of a believer perfected. How often the Christian prays according to the thought in his mind without possessing any revelation in his spirit. He becomes the origin of the prayer himself. But true prayer must originate from the throne of God. It initially is sensed in the person's spirit, next is understood by his mind, and finally is uttered through the power of the Spirit. Man's spirit and prayer are inseparable.

To be able to pray with the spirit a Christian must learn first to walk according to the spirit. No one can pray with his spirit if during the whole day he walks after the flesh. The state of one's prayer life cannot be too greatly disconnected from the condition of his daily walk. The spiritual condition of many too often disqualifies them from praying in the spirit. The quality of a man's prayer is determined by the state of his living. How could a fleshly person offer spiritual prayer? A spiritual person, on the other hand, does not necessarily pray spiritually either, for unless he is watchful he also shall fall into the flesh. Nonetheless, should the spiritual man pray often with his spirit, his very praying shall keep his spirit and mind continually in tune with God. Praying exercises the spirit which in turn is strengthened through such exercising. Negligence in prayer withers the inner man. Nothing can be a substitute for it, not even Christian work. Many are so preoccupied with work that they allow little time for prayer. Hence they cannot cast out demons. Prayer enables us first inwardly to overcome the enemy and then outwardly to deal with him. All who have fought against the enemy on their knees shall see him routed upon their rising up.

Once a believer has contacted the Person of God via the baptism in the Holy Spirit, he then has his own spirit released. He now senses the reality of the things and beings in the spiritual domain. With such knowledge (and let us call to mind that the knowledge of a spiritual man does not accrue to him all at once; some of it may, and usually does, come through many trials), he encounters Satan. Only those who are spiritual perceive the reality of the spiritual foe and hence engage in battle (Ephesians 6.12). Such warfare is not fought with arms of the flesh (2 Corinthians 10.4). Because the conflict is spiritual so must be the weapons. It is a struggle between the spirit of man and that of the enemy—an engagement of spirit with spirit.

SOMETHING TO GUARD AGAINST IN SPIRITUAL WARFARE

Each stage of the believer's walk possesses its particular hazard. The new life within us wages a constant war against all which opposes its growth. During the physical stage, it is a war against sins; in the soulish phase, it is a battle against the natural life; and lastly, on the spiritual level, it is an onslaught against the supernatural enemy. It is solely when a Christian turns spiritual that the evil spirit in that realm launches its assault against his spirit. Accordingly, this is called spiritual warfare. It is fought between spirits and with spirit. Such a phenomenon rarely if ever occurs with unspiritual believers. Do not imagine for a moment, therefore, that when one actually reaches the spiritual plateau he is beyond conflict. A Christian life is an unending engagement on the battlefield. The Christian has no possibility of laying down his arms until he stands before the Lord. While soulish, he faces conflict with the flesh and its danger; when spiritual, he encounters spiritual warfare and its peculiar hazards. Initially there is the war against Amalek in the wilderness. Upon entering Canaan there is next the struggle against the seven tribes of Canaan, wherein the attack of Satan and his evil hosts against the believer's spirit is mounted only after the believer has become spiritual.

Since the enemy focuses particular attention on the spirit, how necessary for spiritual believers to keep their own spirit in its normal state and frequently to exercise it as well. They must control with utmost caution all bodily sensations and carefully distinguish all natural and supernatural phenomena. Their mind must be kept perfectly calm without any disturbance; their physical senses too must be maintained in quiet balance without agitation. Spiritual Christians should exercise their will to deny and oppose any falsehood and seek to follow the inner man with their whole heart. Should they at any time follow the soul instead of the inner man they have lost precious ground already in spiritual warfare. Furthermore, they must be very careful to guard their spirit from being passive in this warfare.

A fundamental difference obtains between the work of the Holy Spirit and that of the evil spirit. *The Holy Spirit moves people themselves to work, never setting aside man's personality; the evil spirit demands men to be entirely inactive so that he may work in their place, reducing man's spirit to a robot.* Hence a passive spirit not only provides the evil one an opportunity to function but binds the hand of the Holy Spirit as well, because He will not operate without the cooperation of the believer. Under these circumstances the evil power inevitably will attempt to exploit the situation. Before a Christian becomes spiritual he is not confronted by this danger of contacting the satanic power; but once he becomes spiritual the wicked one naturally will assault his inner man. The fleshly Christian never experiences this passivity of spirit; the spiritual alone encounters the hazard of developing an errant spirit.

LESSON NINETEEN

INTUITION

For what person knows a man's thoughts except the spirit of the man which is in him.

1 Corinthians 2.11

To understand more clearly what spiritual life is we must analyze the spirit explicitly and assimilate all its laws. Only after we are really acquainted with its different functions are we able to know the laws which govern them; only after we become familiar with those laws can we walk according to the spirit; that is, according to the laws of the spirit. This is indispensable for experiencing the spiritual life. We should never fear appropriating too much knowledge concerning the spirit; but we should be extremely apprehensive if we use our mind excessively in such pursuit.

THE FUNCTIONS OF THE SPIRIT

Mention was made previously that the functions of the spirit could be classified as intuition, communion, and conscience. While these three *can* be distinguished, still, they are closely entwined. It is therefore difficult to treat of one without touching upon the others. When we talk for example about intuition, we naturally must include communion and conscience in our discussion. Thus in dissecting the spirit we necessarily must look into its triple functions. Since we have seen already how the spirit comprises these three abilities, we shall proceed next to uncover what these exactly are in order that we may be helped to walk according to the spirit. We may say that such a walk is a walk by intuition, communion and conscience.

These three are merely the *functions* of the spirit. (Furthermore, they are not the *only* ones; according to the Bible, they are but the *main* functions of the spirit). None of

97

them *is* the spirit, for the spirit itself is substantial, personal, invisible. It is beyond our present comprehension to apprehend the substance of the spirit. What we today know of its substance comes via its various manifestations in us. We will not attempt here to solve future mysteries but only attempt to discover spiritual life; sufficient for us is the knowledge of these abilities or functions and of the way to follow the spirit. Our spirit is not material and yet it exists independently in our body. It must therefore possess its own spiritual substance, out of which arise various abilities for the performance of God's demands on man. Hence what we desire to learn is not the substance but the functions of the spirit.

INTUITION

As the soul has its senses, so too has the spirit. The spirit is intimately related to the soul and yet is wholly unlike it. The soul possesses various senses; but a spiritual man is able to detect another set of senses—lodged in the innermost part of his being—which is radically dissimilar from his set of soulical senses. There in that innermost recess he can rejoice, grieve, anticipate, love, fear, approve, condemn, decide, discern. These motions are sensed in the spirit and are quite distinct from those expressed by the soul through the body.

This spiritual sensing is called "intuition," for it impinges *directly* without reason or cause. Without passing through any procedure, it comes forth in a *straight* manner. Man's ordinary sensing is caused or brought out by people or things or events. We rejoice when there is reason to rejoice, grieve if there is justification to grieve and so forth. Each of these senses has its respective antecedent; hence we cannot conclude them to be expressions of intuition or direct sense. Spiritual sense, on the other hand, does not require any outside cause but emerges directly from within man.

Great similarities do exist between the soul and the spirit. But believers should not walk according to the soul, that is, they should not follow its thoughts, feelings and desires. The way God ordains for His children is a walk after the spirit; all other paths belong to the old creation and hence possess no spiritual value. But how to walk after the spirit? It is living by its intuition because the latter expresses the thought of the spirit which in turn expresses the mind of God.

Oftentimes we think of a certain thing we have good reason to do and our heart delights in it and finally our will decides to execute it; yet somehow, in the inner sanctuary of our being there seems to arise an *unuttered and soundless voice* strongly opposing what our mind, emotion or volition has entertained, felt, or decided. This strange complex seems to infer that this thing ought not to be done. Now such an experience as this may change according to altered conditions. For at other times we may sense in the inner depths that same wordless and noiseless monitor greatly urging, moving and constraining us to perform a certain thing which we view as highly unreasonable, as contrary to what we usually do or desire, and as something which we do not like to do.

THE ANOINTING OF GOD

The intuition of which we have been speaking is exactly the locus (center) where occurs the anointing that teaches: "you have been anointed by the Holy One, and you all *know*. . . But the anointing which you received from him *abides in you*, and you have *no need that any one should teach you*; as his anointing teaches you about everything, and is true, and is no lie, just as it has taught you, abide in him" (1 John 2.20, 27). This portion of Scripture informs us quite lucidly where and how the anointing of the Holy Spirit teaches us.

But before we delve into this passage may we first explain the meaning of "knowing" and "understanding." We usually do not make a distinction between these two words; in spiritual matters, however, the difference between them is incalculable: the spirit "knows" while the mind "understands." A believer "knows" the things of God by the intuition of his spirit. Strictly speaking, the mind can merely "understand"; it can never "know." Knowing is the work of intuition; understanding, the task of the mind. The Holy Spirit enables our spirit to know; our spirit instructs the mind to understand. It may appear difficult to distinguish these two in the abstract, but they are as disparate as wheat from weed in experience. So ignorant are modern believers in their quest to know the thought of the Holy Spirit that they do not even realize how to distinguish "knowing" from "understanding."

Is it not true that we frequently experience this indescribable sense within us which makes us *know* whether or not to do a certain thing? We may say we know the mind of the Holy Spirit in our spirit. Nevertheless our mind may still fail to *understand* what the meaning of it all is. In spiritual matters it is possible for us to know without understanding it. Are there not times when, reaching our wit's end, we receive the teaching of the Holy Spirit in our spirit and jubilantly shout "I know it!"? And are there not times when our mind receives light and understands what the Holy Spirit has meant *long after* we have obeyed and acted on what He has expressed in our intuition? Do we not at that moment exclaim "*Now* I understand it"? These experiences show us that we "know" God's thought in our spirit's intuition but "understand" His guidance in the mind of our soul.

DISCERNMENT

Reading the context of this same portion of Scripture reveals how the Apostle is concerned with many false teachings and antichrists. He assures his readers that the same Holy One Who anoints them also teaches them to differentiate truth from lies and what is of Christ from what is of the antichrists. Christians do not require other men to instruct them since the indwelling Anointing teaches them everything. This is spiritual discernment, something greatly needed today.

If we must pore over many theological references and reason, compare, research, observe and think with our mind until we ultimately reach an understanding of what is lie or what is truth, then only Christians with good minds and education would escape deception. But God has no respect for the old creation; He concludes that all except the newly created spirit must die and be destroyed. Can the wisdom which God demands to be destroyed assist people to know good and evil? No, most emphatically no! God puts His Spirit in every believer's spirit, regardless how sinful or dull he is. The indwelling Spirit shall teach him what is of God and what is not. This is why sometimes we can conjure up no logical reason for opposing a certain teaching, yet in the very depth of our being arises a resistance. We cannot explain it, but our inner sense tells us this is an error. Or contrarily we may hear some teaching which is entirely different from what we generally hold and which we will not like to follow, but is there not occasionally a still small voice that speaks persistently within us and contends that this is the way, walk you in it? Though we may muster many arguments against it, even overwhelming it with reason, nevertheless this inner small voice still insists that we are wrong.

REVELATION

To know things in our intuition is what the Bible calls revelation. Revelation has no other meaning than that the Holy Spirit enables a believer to apprehend a particular matter by indicating the reality of it to his spirit. There is but one kind of knowledge concerning either the Bible or God which is valuable, and that is the truth revealed to our spirit by God's Spirit. God does not explain Himself via man's reasoning; never does man come to know God through rationalization. No matter how clever man's mind is nor how much it understands about God, his knowledge of God remains veiled. All he can do is rationalize what is behind the veil, because he has not penetrated the reality hidden from view. Since he has not yet "seen," man can "understand" but never can he "know." If there is no revelation, personal revelation, Christianity is worth nothing. Everyone who believes in God must have His revelation in his spirit, or else what he believes is not God but mere human wisdom, ideals or words. Such a faith cannot endure the test.

GOD'S WAY OF GUIDING

As at the beginning a believer acquires his first knowledge of God in his spirit, even so must he continue to know God in his spirit. In a Christian life nothing is of any spiritual benefit unless it flows from revelation in the intuition. Whatever does not issue from the spirit is not of God's will. Whatever we think or feel or decide, if not preceded by revelation in the spirit, is reckoned as dead in the eyes of God. Should a believer follow his sudden thought, the "burning fire" in his heart, his natural inclination, his perfect reason, or his rationalization, he is but activating his old man again. God's will is not to be so known; He reveals Himself solely to man's spirit. What is not revealed there is purely human activity.

The revelation of God in our spirit is of two kinds: the direct and the sought. By direct revelation we mean that God, having a particular wish for the believer to do, draws nigh and reveals it to the latter's spirit. Upon receiving such a revelation in his intuition the believer acts accordingly. By sought revelation we mean that a believer, having a special need, approaches God with that need and seeks and waits for an answer through God's movement in his spirit. The revelation young believers receive is mostly the sought type; that of the more matured ones is chiefly the direct kind. We should quickly add, however, that these are not exclusively so, only predominantly so. There lies the difficulty with the young believer. While he ought to wait before the Lord, denying his thought, feeling and desire, he often becomes impatient waiting for His revelation and substitutes his own disguised will for that of God. As a consequence he falls under the accusation of his conscience. Granted that he genuinely has a heart to follow God's intent, he nonetheless unwittingly follows the thought of his mind because he lacks spiritual knowledge. Who can avoid mistakes if he walks without revelation?

Now we find true spiritual knowledge in this: only what is appropriated in the spirit is spiritual knowledge; the rest is wholly the mental kind. Let us inquire a moment, how does God know things? How does He make His judgment? By what knowledge does He control the universe? Does He ascertain with His mind like man? Does He need to think carefully before He understands? Does God depend upon philosophy, logic and comparison to know a matter? Must He search and investigate before He hits upon the solution? Is the Almighty compelled to rely upon His brain? Decidedly not. God has no necessity to indulge in such sweating exercises. His knowledge and judgment is intuitive. As a matter of fact intuition is the common faculty of all spiritual beings. The angels obey what they know as God's will intuitively; they do not arrive at a conclusion by way of argument, reason or contemplation. The difference between knowing intuitively and knowing mentally is immeasurable. Upon this very distinction hangs the outcome of spiritual success or defeat. If it had been intended that a believer's action or service was to be governed by rationalization and common sense, no one would ever have attempted to carry out those many glorious spiritual works of the past and the present, because all of them supersede human reasoning. Who would have dared do them if he had not first known God's will intuitively?

LESSON TWENTY

COMMUNION

God is Spirit, and those who worship him must worship in spirit and truth.

John 4.24

We communicate with the material world through the body. We communicate with the spiritual world through the spirit. This communication with the spiritual is not carried on by means of the mind or emotion but through the spirit or its intuitive faculty. It is easy for us to understand the nature of the communion between God and man if we have seen the operation of our intuition. In order to worship and fellowship with God man must possess a nature similar to His. "God is *spirit*, and those who worship him must worship in *spirit* and truth" (John 4.24). There can be no communication between different natures; hence both the unregenerate whose spirit obviously has not been quickened and the regenerate who does not use his spirit to worship are equally unqualified to have genuine fellowship with God. Lofty sentiments and noble feelings do not bring people into spiritual reality nor do they forge personal communion with God. Our fellowship with Him is experienced in the deepest place of our entire being, deeper than our thought, feeling and will, even in the intuition of our spirit.

A close scrutiny of 1 Corinthians 2.9-3.2 can provide a very clear view of how man communes with God and how man knows the realities of God through the spirit's intuition.

"What no eye has seen, nor ear heard, nor the heart of man conceived, what God has prepared for those who love him" (v.9). The larger context of this one verse speaks of God and the things of God. What He has prepared can neither be seen or heard by man's outward body nor conceived by his inward heart. The "heart of man" includes among other facets man's

104

understanding, mind and intellect. Man's thought cannot envisage God's work, for the latter transcends the former. It is therefore evident that he who desires to know and commune with God cannot depend solely upon his thought.

THE HOLY SPIRIT

"God has revealed to us through the Spirit. For the Spirit searches everything; even the depths of God" (v.10). This verse sets forth the fact that the *Holy Spirit searches* everything and not that our mind conceives all. Only the Holy Spirit knows the depths of God. He knows what man does not know. By His intuition the Spirit searches everything. God is thus able to reveal through Him what our heart has never conceived. This "revealing" is not acquired after much thinking, for our heart cannot even conceive it. It is a revelation; it does not require the help of our thought.

The next two verses tell us how God reveals Himself. "For what person knows a man's thoughts except the spirit of the man which is in him? So also no one comprehends the thoughts of God except the Spirit of God. Now we have received not the spirit of the world, but the Spirit which is from God, that we might understand the gifts bestowed on us by God" (vv.11 and 12). No one knows man's thoughts except the spirit of man; likewise, no one knows the things of God but the Holy Spirit. Man's spirit as well as God's Spirit apprehend things directly, not by deducing or searching. They perceive through the faculty of intuition. Since the Holy Spirit alone knows the things of God, we must receive the Holy Spirit if we also would know those things. The spirit of the world is cut off from communication with God. It is a dead spirit: it cannot effect communion with Him. The Holy Spirit, on the other hand, comprehends the things of God; therefore, by receiving in our intuition what the Holy Spirit knows, we too shall understand the realities of God. "We have received ... the

Spirit which is from God, that we might understand the gifts bestowed on us by God."

How then do *we know*? Verse 11 tells us man knows by his spirit. The Holy Spirit unfolds to our spirit what He knows intuitively so that we too may know intuitively. When the Holy Spirit discloses the matters pertaining to God He does so not to our mind nor to any other organ but to our spirit. God knows this is the sole place in man which can apprehend man's things as well as His things. The mind is not the place for knowing these think and conceive many matters, it nonetheless cannot *know* things. While it is true that the mind can them.

From this we can appreciate how highly God esteems the regenerated spirit of man. Before new birth man's spirit was dead. God had no way of unfolding His mind to such a man. The cleverest brain fails to know the mind of God. Both God's fellowship with man and man's worship of God are contingent upon the regenerated spirit of man. Without this revitalized component God and man are hopelessly separated—neither can come or go to the other. The first step towards communion between God and man must be this quickening of man's spirit.

THE SPIRIT OF WISDOM AND REVELATION

In our communion with God the spirit of wisdom and revelation is imperative. "The God of our Lord Jesus Christ, the Father of glory, may give you a spirit of wisdom and of revelation in the knowledge of him" (Ephesians 1.17). When a new spirit is received at regeneration its functions await development, for they presently lie dormant there. The Apostle Paul prayed for the regenerated believers at Ephesus, desiring that they receive the spirit of wisdom and revelation so that they might know God intuitively. Whether this ability is a hidden function of the believer's spirit which is activated through prayer or whether it is something added by the Holy Spirit to the believer's spirit as a result of prayer, we do not know. Yet one thing is certain: this spirit of wisdom and revelation is essential to one's communion with God. We also recognize that it can be obtained through prayer.

CONSCIENCE

How much more shall the blood of Christ, who through the eternal Spirit offered himself without blemish to God, purify your conscience from dead works to serve the living God.

Hebrews 9.14

Besides the functions of intuition and communion, our spirit performs still another important task—that of correcting and reprimanding so as to render us uneasy when we fall short of the glory of God. This ability we call conscience. As the holiness of God condemns evil and justifies good, so a believer's conscience reproves sin and approves righteousness. Conscience is where God expresses His holiness. If we desire to follow the spirit (and since we never reach a stage of infallibility), we must heed what our inward monitor tells us regarding both inclination and overt action. For its works would be decidedly incomplete if it were only *after* we have committed error that conscience should rise up to reprove us. But we realize that even before we take any step—while we are still considering our way—our conscience together with our intuition will protest immediately and make us uneasy at any thought or inclination which is displeasing to the Holy Spirit. If we were more disposed today to mind the voice of conscience we would not be as defeated as we are.

CONSCIENCE AND SALVATION

While we were sinners our spirit was thoroughly dead; our conscience was therefore dead as well and unable to function normally. This does not mean the conscience of a sinner stops working altogether. It does continue to operate, though in a state of coma. Whenever it comes out of this coma it does nothing but condemn the sinner. It has no strength to lead men to God. Dead as it is to Him, God nonetheless desires the conscience to perform some feeble work in the heart of man. Hence in man's dead spirit conscience appears to do a little more work than the other functions of the spirit. The death of intuition and of communion seems to be a greater one than that of conscience. There is of course a reason for the variation. As soon as Adam ate the fruit of the tree of the knowledge of good and evil his intuition and communion died completely towards God, but his power of distinguishing good and evil (which is the function of conscience) was increased. Even today, while the intuition and communion of a sinner are altogether dead to God, his conscience retains something of its movement. This does not imply that man's conscience is alive; for according to the Biblical meaning of aliveness only that which has the life of God is reckoned as living. Anything void of God's life is considered dead. Since the conscience of a sinner does not embrace the life of God it is accounted dead, though it may appear to be active according to man's feeling. Such activity of the conscience augments the anguish of a sinner.

In initiating His work of salvation the first step of the Holy Spirit is to awaken this comatose conscience. He uses the thunders and lightnings of Mount Sinai to shake and enlighten this darkened conscience so as to convince the sinner of his violation of God's law and of his inability to answer God's righteous demand and additionally to convict him as one who is condemned and who deserves nothing but perdition. If one's conscience is willing to confess whatever sins have been committed, including the sin of unbelief, it will be sorrowful in a godly way, earnestly desiring the mercy of God. The tax-collector in our Lord's parable who went up to the temple to pray illustrates such a work of the Holy Spirit. It is what the Lord Jesus meant in his statement: "When (the Holy Spirit) comes, he will convince the world of sin and of righteousness and of judgment" (John 16.8). Should a man's conscience be closed to the conviction, however, then he can never be saved.

The Holy Spirit illuminates a sinner's conscience with the light of God's law so as to convict him of sin; the same Spirit also enlightens man's conscience with the light of the gospel so as to save him. If a sinner, upon being convicted of his sin and hearing the gospel of God's grace, is willing to accept the gospel and by faith take it, he will see how the precious blood of the Lord Jesus answers all the accusations of his conscience. Doubtless there is sin, but the blood of the Lord Jesus has been shed. What ground is left for accusation since sin's penalty has been fully paid? The blood of the Lord has atoned for all the sins of a believer; hence there is no more condemnation in the conscience. "If the worshipers had once been cleansed, they would no longer have any consciousness of sin" (Hebrews 10.2). We may stand before God without fear and trembling because the blood of Christ has been sprinkled on our conscience (Hebrews 9.14). Our salvation is confirmed by the fact that the precious blood has quieted this voice of condemnation.

CONSCIENCE AND COMMUNION

"How much more shall the blood of Christ, who through the eternal Spirit offered himself without blemish to God, purify your conscience from dead works to serve the living God" (Hebrews 9.14). In order to commune with God and to serve Him one first must have his conscience cleansed by the precious blood. As a believer's conscience is cleansed he is regenerated. According to the Scriptures the cleansing by the blood and the regeneration of the spirit occur simultaneously. Here we are informed that before one can serve God he must receive a new life and have his intuition quickened through the cleansing of the conscience by the blood. A conscience so cleansed makes it possible for the intuition of the spirit to serve God. Conscience and intuition are inseparable.

"Let *us draw near* with a true heart in full assurance of

110

faith, with our hearts sprinkled clean from an evil conscience and our bodies washed with pure water" (Hebrews 10.22). We do not draw near to God physically as did the people in the Old Testament period, for our sanctuary is in heaven; nor do we draw near soulically with our thoughts and feelings since these organs can never commune with God. The regenerated spirit alone can approach Him. Believers worship God in their quickened intuition. The verse above affirms that a sprinkled conscience is the basis for communion with God intuitively. A conscience tinged with offense is under constant accusation. That naturally will affect the intuition, so closely knit to the conscience, and discourage its approach to God, even paralyzing its normal function. How infinitely necessary to have "a true heart in full assurance of faith" in a believer's communion with God. When conscience is unclear one's approach to Him becomes forced and is not true because he cannot fully believe that God is for him and has nothing against him. Such fear and doubt undermine the normal function of intuition, depriving it of the liberty to fellowship freely with God. The Christian must not have the slightest accusation in his conscience; he must be assured that his every sin is entirely atoned by the blood of the Lord and that now there is no charge against him (Romans 8.33-34). A single offense on the conscience may suppress and suspend the normal function of intuition in communing with God, for as soon as a believer is conscious of sin his spirit gathers all its powers to eliminate that particular sin and leaves no more strength to ascend heavenward.

A BELIEVER'S CONSCIENCE

A believer's conscience is quickened when his spirit is regenerated. The precious blood of the Lord Jesus purifies his conscience and accordingly gives it an acute sense that it should obey the will of the Holy Spirit. The sanctifying work of the Holy Spirit in man and the work of conscience in man are intimately related and mutually joined. If a child of God desires to be filled with the Spirit, to be sanctified, and to lead a life wholly after God's will, he must adhere to the voice of conscience. Should he not grant it its rightful place, he shall fall inescapably into walking after the flesh. To be faithful to one's conscience is the first step toward sanctification. Following its voice is a sign of true spirituality. If a Christian fails to let it do its work he is barred from entering the spiritual realm. Even if he regards himself (and is so regarded by others) as spiritual, his "spirituality" nevertheless lacks foundation. If sin and other matters contrary to God's will and unbecoming to saints are not restrained as dictated by its voice, then whatever has been superimposed through spiritual theory shall ultimately collapse because there is no genuine foundation.

Conscience testifies as to whether we are clear towards God and towards men and as to whether our thoughts, words and deeds follow the will of God and are not in any way rebellious to Christ. As Christians advance spiritually the witness of conscience and the witness of the Holy Spirit seem to close ranks. This is because conscience, being fully under the control of the Holy Spirit, daily grows more sensitive until it is attuned perfectly to the voice of the Spirit. The Latter is thereby able to speak to believers through their consciences. The Apostle's word that "my conscience bears me witness in the Holy Spirit" (Romans 9.1) carries within it this meaning.

A GOOD CONSCIENCE

"Our boast is this, the testimony of our conscience that we have behaved in the world, and still more toward you, with holiness and godly sincerity, not by earthly wisdom but by the grace of God" (2 Corinthians 1.12). This passage speaks of the testimony of conscience. Only a conscience without offense will testify for a believer. It is good to have the testimony of others, but how much better to have the testimony of our own conscience. The Apostle asserts that this is what he is boasting of here. In our walk after the spirit we need to have this testimony continually. What other people say is subject to error because they cannot fully know how God has guided us. Perhaps they may misunderstand and misjudge us just as the Apostles were misunderstood and misjudged by the believers in their day. At times they also may over-praise and over-admire us. Many times men criticize us when we actually are following the Lord; on other occasions they praise us for what they see in us, though it is largely the result of a temporary emotional outburst or a cleverly conceived thought on our part. Hence outside praise or criticism is inconsequential; but the testimony of our quickened conscience is momentous. We should pay extreme attention to how it bears us witness. What is its estimate of us? Does it condemn us as hypocritical? Or does it testify that we have walked among men in holiness and godly sincerity? Does conscience affirm that we already have walked according to all the light we have?

CONSCIENCE AND KNOWLEDGE

In abiding by the spirit and listening to the voice of conscience we should remember one thing, and that is, conscience is limited by knowledge. It is the organ for distinguishing good and evil, which means it gives us the knowledge of good and evil. This knowledge varies with different Christians. Some have more while others have less. The degree of knowledge may be determined by individual environment or perhaps by the instruction each has received. Thus we can neither live by the standard of others nor ask other people to live by the light we have. In a Christian's fellowship with God an unknown sin does not hinder communion. Whoever observes all the will of God known to him and forsakes everything known to be condemned by God is qualified to enjoy perfect fellowship with Him. A young Christian frequently concludes that due to his lack of knowledge he is powerless to please God. *Spiritual* knowledge is indeed quite important, but we also know that the lack of such knowledge does not hinder one's fellowship with God. In the matter of fellowship God looks not at how much we apprehend of His will but rather at what our *attitude* towards His will is. If we honestly seek and wholeheartedly obey His desires, our fellowship remains unbroken, even though there should be many unknown sins in us. Should fellowship be determined by the holiness of God, who among all the most holy saints in the past and the present would be qualified to hold a moment's perfect communion with Him? Everyone would be banished daily from the Lord's face and from the glory of His might. That sin which is unknown to us is under the covering of the precious blood.

On the other hand, were we to permit to remain even the tiniest little sin which we know our conscience has condemned, we instantly would lose that perfect fellowship with God. Just as a speck of dust disables us from seeing, so our known sin, no matter how infinitesimal, hides God's smiling face from us. The moment the conscience is offended immediately fellowship is affected. A sin unknown to the saint may persist long in his life without affecting his fellowship with God; but as soon as light (knowledge) breaks in, he forfeits a day's fellowship with Him for every day he allows that sin to remain. God fellowships with us according to the level of the knowledge of our conscience. We shall be very foolish if we assume that, since a certain matter has not hindered our fellowship with God for so many years, it cannot later be of any consequence.

LESSON TWENTY-TWO

THE DANGERS OF SPIRITUAL LIFE

Work out your salvation with fear and trembling.

Philippians 2.12b

There are countless Christians who consider the occasional working of the Holy Spirit in their spirit to be the most sublime of their life experiences. They do not expect to have such an experience daily because they surmise that such a special event could happen but a few times in life. Were they to live by the spirit according to its law, however, they would discover that these are everyday occurrences. What they deem extraordinary—something one cannot permanently sustain—is actually the *ordinary* daily experiences of believers. "Extraordinary" indeed if believers should desert this ordinary life experience and abide in darkness.

We know our soul provides us with self-consciousness. One aspect of self-consciousness is self-examination. This is most harmful since it causes us to focus upon ourselves and thereby enhance the growth of self life. How often self-exaltation and pride are the consequences of such self-examination. But there is a kind of analysis of incalculable help to the spiritual pilgrimage. Without it we are incompetent to know who we really are and what we are following. Harmful self-examination revolves around one's own success or defeat, stimulating attitudes of self-pride or self-pity. Profitable analysis searches only the *source* of one's thought, feeling or desire. God wishes us to be delivered from self-consciousness, but at the same time He certainly does not intend for us to live on earth as people without intelligent awareness. We must not be overly self-conscious, yet we must apprehend the true condition of all our inward parts through the knowledge accorded us by the Holy Spirit. It is positively necessary for us to search out our activities with our heart.

Now as a matter of fact the sense of the soul and the intuition of the spirit are distinctly opposite; nevertheless, occasionally they appear to be quite similar. Their similarity can be so close as to confuse Christians. Should they be hasty to move, they will not easily escape being deceived at these times of similarity. Yet if they would wait patiently and test the source of their feelings again and again, they would be told the real source by the Holy Spirit at the right hour. In walking after the spirit we must avoid all haste.

THE ATTACKS OF SATAN

In view of the significance of our spirit, which is the site of communion between the Holy Spirit and the saints, should we marvel if Satan is most unwilling to let us know the functions of the spirit for fear we may follow it? The enemy aims to confine the saint's life within the soul and to quench his spirit. He will give many strange physical sensations to believers and fill their mind with various wandering thoughts. He intends to confuse one's spiritual awareness by these sensations and thoughts. While confused, God's children are incompetent to distinguish what is of the spirit and what emanates from the soul. Satan well recognizes that victories of believers rest in their knowing how to "read" their spiritual sense (alas! how many are ignorant of this principle). He musters his whole force to attack the believer's spirit.

Satan employs even more drastic measures against believers than that of enticing them into living by the soul instead of following the spirit. Upon succeeding in luring them—through their thoughts or feelings—to live by the outward man, Satan adopts the next step of pretending to be a spirit in them. He will create many deceptive feelings in the believers in order to confuse their spiritual senses. If they are ignorant of the wiles of the enemy, they just may allow their spirit to be suppressed until it ceases to function. And then they heed this counterfeit feeling as though they were still following the spirit. Once their spiritual sense grows dull, Satan proceeds further in his deceit. He injects into their minds the thought that now God is leading them by their renewed mind, thus subtly covering up the fault of men in *not using* their spirit as well as covering up the work of the enemy. As soon as man's spirit ceases to operate, the Holy Spirit can no longer find any cooperative element within him; naturally then, all resources from God are cut off. And it is hence impossible for such ones to continue to experience true spiritual life.

Spiritual ones ought to possess spiritual knowledge so that all their movements can be governed by spiritual reasoning. They should not act impulsively according to fleeting emotion or flashing thought. They should never be in haste. Every action must be scrutinized with spiritual insight in order that only what is approved by the spirit's intuitive knowledge is permitted. Nothing should be done which is propelled by excited feeling or abrupt thought; everything must be carefully and quietly examined before it is executed.

THE ACCUSATION OF SATAN

Satan has another way to assault those who set their heart on following the leading of the spirit's intuition. This is by counterfeiting or falsely representing one's conscience with all sorts of accusations. To keep our conscience pure we are willing to accept its reproach and deal with whatever it condemns. The enemy utilizes this desire of keeping the conscience void of offense by accusing us of various things. In mistaking such accusations as being from our own consciences we often lose our peace, tire of trying to keep pace with the false accusations, and thus cease to advance spiritually with confidence.

Those who are spiritual ought to be aware that Satan not only indicts us before God but also to ourselves. He does this to disturb us into thinking we ought to suffer penalty because we have done wrong. He is alert to the fact that the children of God can make no progress spiritually unless they have a heart full of confidence; consequently he falsifies the accusation of conscience in order to make them believe they have sinned. Then their communion with God is broken. The problem with believers is that they do not know how to distinguish between the indictment of the evil spirit and the reproach of conscience. Frequently out of fear of offending God, they mistake the accusation of an evil spirit to be the censure of conscience. This accusation grows stronger and stronger until it becomes uncontrollable. Thus in addition to their willingness to yield to conscience's reproof, spiritual believers should also learn how to discern the accusation of the enemy.

What the enemy charges the saints of may sometimes be real sins, though more often than not they are merely imaginary—that is, the evil spirit makes them *feel* they have sinned. If they actually *have* sinned, they should confess it immediately before God, asking for the cleansing of the precious blood (1 John 1.9). Yet should the accusing voice still continue, it obviously must be from the evil spirit.

ADDITIONAL DANGERS

Other hazards lie in the way of following the spirit besides Satan's counterfeits and his attacks. Often our soul will fabricate or sense something which urges us to take action. Christians must never forget that not all senses emerge from the spirit, for the body, the soul, and the spirit each has its own senses. It is highly important not to interpret soulical or physical senses as the intuition of the spirit. God's children should learn daily in experience what is and what is not genuine intuition. How very easy for us, once perceiving the importance of following the intuition, to overlook the fact that senses exist in other parts of the being besides in the spirit. Actually spiritual life is neither so complicated nor so easy as people usually imagine.

Here then are two causes for alarm: first, the peril of mistaking other senses to be the spirit's intuition; and second, the danger of misunderstanding the meaning of intuition. We meet these two hazards every day. Hence the teaching of the Holy Scriptures is quite essential. To confirm whether or not we are moved by, and walk in, the Holy Spirit, we must see if any given thing harmonizes with the teaching of the Bible. The Holy Spirit never moves the prophets of old to write in one way and then move us today in another way. It is categorically impossible for the Holy Spirit to have instructed people of yesteryear what they ought not to do and yet tell us in our day that we must do these very same things. What we receive in the spirit's intuition needs to be certified by the teaching of God's Word. To follow intuition alone and not in conjunction with the Scriptures will *undeniably* lead us into error. The revelation of the Holy Spirit sensed by our spirit must coincide with the revelation of the Holy Spirit in Scripture.

One more matter needs to be noticed: a great danger looms before us if we live and walk by the spirit too much. Although the Word does emphasize the believer's personal spirit, the Word also informs us that the significance of one's spirit is due to the indwelling *Holy Spirit*. The reason why we must walk and live in the spirit at all is because our spirit, being the habitation of God's Spirit, is where He expresses His mind. The leading and discipline we receive therein is His leading and discipline. In stressing the significance of the Holy Spirit we are at the same time emphasizing our own spirit since the latter constitutes His base of operation. Our danger, upon apprehending the work and function of man's spirit, is to rely entirely on it, forgetting that it is merely the servant of the Holy Spirit. God's Spirit and not our spirit is the One upon Whom we wait for direct guidance into all truth. If man's spirit is divorced from the divine Spirit it becomes as useless as the other parts of man. We should never reverse the order of man's spirit and the Holy Spirit. It is because many of the

Lord's people are ignorant of man's spirit and its operation that we have presented in these pages a detailed account of it. This does not mean, however, that the position of the Holy Spirit in a man is inferior to that of his own spirit. The purpose for understanding this faculty of man is to help us to obey Him more and to exalt Him more.

THE LAWS OF THE SPIRIT

For the law of the Spirit of life in Christ Jesus has set you free from the law of sin and of death.

Romans 8.2 (NASV)

A child of God must learn to recognize the sense of consciousness of his inner being as the first condition for a life walked after the spirit. If he does not discern what is the sense of the spirit and additionally the sense of the soul, he invariably shall fail to do what the spirit requires of him. For instance, when we feel hungry we know we should eat; when we feel cold we know we should be clothed. Our senses express needs and requirements. We must therefore know what our physical senses mean before we can know how to satisfy them with material supplies. In the spiritual realm, too, one must come to understand the meanings of his spirit's various senses as well as their respective supply. Only after an individual comprehends his spirit with its movements can he walk by the spirit.

There are a few laws of the spirit with which every Christian ought to be acquainted. If he does not understand these laws or fails to see the significance of recognizing the sensations of the spirit, he will miss many of its movements. His failure to discern its senses undermines the proper place of the spirit in his daily walk. Hence once we have known the various functions of the inner man, such as intuition, communion and conscience, we need to identify their movements which can then enable us to walk by the spirit. Being filled with the Holy Spirit, our spirit will be operating actively. But we shall incur loss if we disregard these operations. It is thus imperative that we observe the way the spirit habitually moves. A Christian should know more about the operation of his spirit than about the activity of his mind.

(1) WEIGHTS ON THE SPIRIT

The spirit needs to be kept in a state of perfect freedom. It should always be light, as though floating in the air; only so may life grow and work be done. A Christian ought to realize what the weights laid on his spirit are. Often he feels it is under oppression, as if a thousand pound load were pressing upon his heart. He can unearth no reason for this weight, which usually steals in upon one quite suddenly. It is employed by the enemy to harass the spiritual, to deprive him of joy and lightness, as well as to disable his spirit from working together with the Holy Spirit. If he does not recognize the source of this heaviness and the meaning of the oppression in the spirit, he cannot instantly deal with it and thereby restore his spirit immediately to normalcy.

(2) BLOCKAGE OF THE SPIRIT

The spirit requires the soul and body as organs for expression. It is like a mistress who must have a steward and a servant working for her to accomplish her wish. It can also be likened to an electric current which requires wire to show forth light. Should the soul and body lose their normality under the attack of the enemy, the spirit shall be shut in and denied any means of outlet. The adversary is familiar with the requirements of the spirit; therefore he frequently acts against the believer's soul and body. When these parts cease to function properly the spirit is stripped of its means of expression and so forfeits its victorious position.

During such a period one's mind may be confused, his emotions disturbed, his will weary and impotent to actively govern the whole being, or his body overly tired and temporarily lazy. He must resist these symptoms at once or else his spirit will be blocked in and he be unfit either to engage the enemy livingly in battle or to retain his ground of victory.

(3) POISONING OF THE SPIRIT

Our spirit can be poisoned by the evil spirit. This poison is the flaming dart of the enemy, aimed directly at our spirit. Into it he shoots sorrow, grief, anguish, woe or heartbreak to cause us to have a "sorrowful spirit" (1 Samuel 1.15 ASV): and a "broken spirit who can bear?" (Proverbs 18.14) It is exceedingly hazardous for anyone to accept without objection or question every sorrow which comes upon him and take for granted that these are naturally his own feelings. He has not yet examined the source nor put up any resistance. Let us remember to never accept any thought or feeling lightly. If we wish to walk after the spirit we must be watchful in all points, searching especially the source of every notion and sensation.

Sometimes Satan provokes us to harden our spirit. It can become stiff, unyielding, narrow and selfish. Such a spirit cannot work with God nor can it do His will. And so a believer will abandon his love towards men; he will shed every delicate, sympathetic, tenderhearted feeling towards others. Since he has lost the generosity of the Lord and has drawn a circle around himself, how can the Holy Spirit ever use him mightily?

The evil spirit infects the believer's spirit with these and other venoms. If these poisons are not opposed instantly they soon become "the works of the flesh" (Galatians 5.19). At first these are only poisons from Satan, but they can be transformed into sins of the flesh if the Christian accepts them, even unconsciously, rather than resists them.

In ordinary times the Lord's people should early take the shield of faith which quenches all the flaming darts of the evil one. This implies that we should swiftly exercise living faith to look for God's protection and to withstand the enemy's attack. Faith is our shield, not our extractor: faith is a weapon for quenching the flaming darts, not for pulling them out afterwards. But should anyone be hit by a flaming dart, he at once must eliminate the cause of the dart. He should maintain an attitude of resistance, immediately denying whatever comes from Satan and praying for cleansing.

(4) SINKING OF THE SPIRIT

The spirit sinking or being submerged is largely due to a turning in on oneself. It may be induced by a possessiveness over all the experiences one has had or by an intrusion of the power of darkness or by a self-centeredness in prayer and worship. When anyone's spirit is tilted inward instead of outward the power of God is at once severed and the spirit will soon be surrounded by the soul.

Sometimes this submerging of the spirit in the soul is precipitated by the deceit of the evil foe who supplies the person with physical sensations and various wonderful joyful experiences. He does not perceive that they originate with the evil spirit: he instead construes them to be from God: and thus he unknowingly comes to dwell in a sensuous world where his spirit is drowned in the soul.

(5) BURDENS OF THE SPIRIT

The burdens of the spirit differ from the weights on the spirit. The latter proceed from Satan with the intent of crushing the believer and making him suffer, but the former issue from God in His desire to manifest His will to the believer so that he may cooperate with Him. Any weight on the spirit has no other objective than to oppress; it therefore usually serves no purpose and produces no fruit. A burden of the spirit, on the other hand, is given by God to His child for the purpose of calling him to work, to pray, or to preach. It is a burden with purpose, with reason, and for spiritual profit. We must learn how to distinguish the burden of the spirit from the weight on the spirit.

(6) EBBING OF THE SPIRIT

God's life and power in our spirit can recede like a tide. We recognize that anyone soulish usually deems his spiritual life to be at high tide when he *feels* the presence of God; but if he feels low and dry, he is at ebb tide. These are of course but feelings; they do not represent the reality of spiritual life.

Immediately upon sensing a waning in his spiritual life, a child of God automatically should realize an obstruction must exist somewhere. Satan will accuse you of having retrogressed spiritually; other people will judge you as having lost power; and you yourself will imagine you must have committed some grave sin. These may be true, but they do not form the whole truth. Actually, such a situation is *mostly*, though not entirely, created because of our not knowing how to cooperate with God in fulfilling His conditions for the certainty of a ceaseless flow. Foolishness is a prime factor. Hence a person should immediately pray and meditate over, and test and search out the cause for, such an ebbing. He should wait upon God, asking His Spirit to reveal the reason. In the meantime, he should try to unearth where he has failed to fulfill the condition for the steady flow of life.

(7) IRRESPONSIBILITY OF THE SPIRIT

Man's spirit can be compared to an electric bulb. When in contact with the Holy Spirit, it shines; but should it be disconnected, it plunges into darkness. "The spirit of man is the lamp of the Lord" (Proverbs 20.27). God's aim is to fill the human spirit with light; yet the believer's spirit is sometimes darkened. Why is this? It is because it has lost contact with the Holy Spirit. To perceive whether or not one's spirit is connected with the Holy Spirit, one need only notice if it is shining.

We have said before that God's Spirit dwells in man's and that he cooperates with Him through his own spirit. If the spirit of man has been deprived of its normal condition it will seem to be disconnected from the Holy Spirit, losing all its light. It thus is very necessary for us to maintain our spirit in a healthy quiet state so as to insure its cooperation with the Holy Spirit. If it is disturbed by external forces it automatically is bereft of its power to cooperate with the Holy Spirit and is plunged into darkness.

Once realizing his spirit has been irresponsible, a believer should oppose without delay all the works of the enemy as well as the causes for the enemy's work. Should it be purely the attack of the adversary the spirit will regain its freedom after having resisted. But if there is justification for the attack, that is, if the person has given any ground to the enemy, then he must uncover the reason and deal with it. Usually the reason is related to the past history of the individual. He needs to pray over such various matters as his environment, family, relatives, friends, work, and so forth. When his spirit senses a release after a certain matter has been prayed over, then he has isolated the cause for the enemy's assault. Shortly after he has taken care of this matter, the believer's spirit will be freed and restored to its function.

(8) CONDITIONS OF THE SPIRIT

Let us summarize. A believer should know every law of the spirit if he desires to live by it. If he is not vigilant and loses the cooperation of his spirit with God, then he unquestionably has fallen. To discern the particular condition of his inner man is one of the most central laws pertaining to the spirit. All which we have discussed in the chapter are included in this law.

A child of God ought to know what is and what is not the normal condition for his spirit. Since it should have authority over man's soul and body, occupying the highest position in him and possessing the greatest power, the Christian needs to know if such is the situation in him or not. He should also recognize whether his spirit, if it has lost its normalcy, did so through war or environment. The conditions of the spirit may be classified generally into four types:

(a) The spirit is oppressed and is therefore in decline.

(b) The spirit is under compulsion and so is forced into inordinate activity.

(c) The spirit is defiled (2 Corinthians 7.1) since it has yielded ground to sin.

(d) The spirit is quiet and firm because it occupies its rightful position.

LESSON TWENTY-FOUR

THE PRINCIPLE OF MIND AIDING THE SPIRIT

And do not be conformed to this world, but be transformed by the renewing of your mind, so that you may prove what the will of God is, that which is good and acceptable and perfect.

Romans 12.2 (NASV)

There is something else of no less importance for anyone wishing to walk after the spirit: the principle of the mind aiding or assisting it. This principle is to be applied constantly. Many defeats in spiritual life can be traced to ignorance of it, even though the laws of the spirit are indeed known. And why? Because these laws can only explain to us the meaning of the spirit's stirring and supply us with ways to satisfy their particular demands. Whenever the spirit senses anything, we are equipped by the knowledge of these laws to fulfill the requirement called for; if the condition is normal, we walk accordingly; and if abnormal, we can correct it. But a problem arises here; which is, that we do not always enjoy such spiritual stirrings. The spirit simply may not speak. Many have experienced an utter silence for quite a few days. It appears as though it is sleeping. Is this to say that during those days when our spirit is inactive we should do nothing? Must we quietly sit for a number of days, neither praying nor reading the Bible nor performing any work? Our spiritual common sense vigorously replies: no, by no means should we waste the time. But if we do anything during that period will it not mean that we labor in the power of the flesh and not according to the spirit?

Now this is just the moment when we should apply the principle of the mind supporting the spirit. But how? When the spirit is sleeping, our mind must come in to do the work of the spirit. And before long we shall see the latter itself joining in

128

the work. The mind and the spirit are closely knit: they are to help each other. Many times the spirit senses something which the mind is made to understand, and then action is taken; while on other occasions the spirit is unmoved and needs to be aroused by the activity of the believer's mind. If the spirit is inactive the mind can induce it to move. And once moved, the believer should follow it. Such inducement of the spirit by the mind is what we here term as the principle or law of the mind aiding the spirit. There is a principle in spiritual life which holds that in the *beginning* we should exercise our spiritual sense to apprehend God-given knowledge, but that afterwards we must keep and use this knowledge by means of the mind. For example, you notice a great need somewhere. According to the knowledge you have received from God, you realize you should pray and petition Him for supply. But at the time you see the need your spirit does not feel at all like praying. What should you do? You should pray with your *mind* instead of waiting for the spirit to move. Every need is a call to prayer. Although at the start you pray despite silence in your spirit, as you pray on you will soon be conscious of something rising within you. It signifies your spirit has joined in at last in this work of prayer.

Occasionally our inner man is so oppressed by Satan or so disturbed by the natural life that we can hardly discern it. It has sunk so low that it seems to have lost its consciousness. We continue to feel the presence of our soul and body, but the spirit appears to be absent. If we should wait for it to stir before we pray, we shall probably never do so, nor shall it regain its freedom. What we must do is pray with what the mind remembers to be the truth we once received and in that prayer resist the power of darkness. If ever we do not sense the spirit we should pray with our mind. Such mental activity eventually will incite our spirit to move.

"Pray(ing) with the mind" (1 Corinthians 14.15) can act- ivate the spirit. Although at the outset we may appear to be praying with empty words, divested of any meaning, nevertheless as we pray along with our mind and resist with prayer our spirit soon will ascend. Whereupon the spirit and the mind will work together. And as soon as it comes in, prayer becomes meaningful and quite free. The cooperation between these two elements delineates the normal state of spiritual life.

INTERCESSION

We all appreciate the importance of intercession. Yet often when we have time to spend in intercession our spirit is inactive and fails to supply us with subjects for intercessory prayer. This does not mean we need not pray on that occasion or that we can utilize the time for other matters. On the contrary, it serves as a hint for us to intercede in prayer with the mind and to hope and expect the spirit will be activated into participating. You should accordingly exercise your mind to remember your friends, relatives, and fellow-workers to determine if they are in need. As you remember each one so shall you in turn intercede for them. If in interceding on their behalf your spirit remains cold and dry, then you know you are not to pray for them. But supposing at that same time you recall a special lack in your local church or a number of temptations the church is facing or certain hindrances to the Lord's work in a particular area or some distinctive truths which God's children ought to know today. In that event you should intercede for each of them as they come to your attention. If after praying awhile over these matters your spirit still fails to respond as you are yet praying with your mind, then you realize once again that these are not what the Lord desires you to pray for today. But supposing as you touch upon certain matters in your prayer you feel as though the Holy Spirit is anointing you and your spirit seems to respond: it is at this singular moment that you recognize you are at last interceding for what is on the Lord's heart. Hence the principle calls for the exercise of the mind to help the spirit locate its trend.

KNOWING GOD'S WILL

God's guidance does not always come to us directly; it is sometimes indirect. In direct guidance the Spirit of God moves in our spirit and so enables us to know His will. If our mind is attentive to the movement in the spirit we shall easily understand the will of God. But in the various affairs of life God does not necessarily tell us many things directly. There may be many needs of which we as men are aware. What should we do about these conscious needs? We may be invited to work somewhere or something else may suddenly happen. Such matters as these obviously are not sponsored directly by our spirit, for they come to us from other people. Our mind sees the urgency of solving these problems, yet our spirit is unresponsive. How may we experience the guidance of God in such a situation? Well, when we encounter something of this kind, we must with our mind ask God to lead us in the spirit. By so doing we are experiencing the indirect guidance of God. This is the moment the mind must assist the spirit. When one notices his spirit is inactive he should exercise his mind. It is not necessary for it to assist if the spirit is exuding its thought incessantly: only as the spirit remains silent must the mind fill the gap for it.

In such circumstances the believer should exercise his mind by pondering this unsolved matter before God. Although such prayer and consideration emerge from his mind, before long his spirit will collaborate in the prayer and consideration. His spirit which he did not sense before he now begins to sense, and soon the Holy Spirit will be found leading him in his spirit. We should never sit back because of a lack of early movement therein. Rather should we use the mind to "scoop up" (stir up) our spirit and activate it to help us know whether or not this matter is of God.

The mind supporting the spirit can be likened to operating a hand water pump. In some pumps it is essential to pour into it a cup of water just to provide suction for the machine while pumping. The relation of our mind to the spirit is similar to that between the cup of water and the water pump. If you do not use this cup of water as a starter you shall be powerless to pump up water from the well. Even so, our spirit will not rise up unless we exercise the mind first. Not to start praying with the mind for the sake of the spirit is like a man who neglects to pour in that cup of water first and concludes after pumping twice that there is not any water in the well.

THE CONDITION OF THE MIND

Inferior though it be to the spirit, the mind nonetheless can assist it. Besides bolstering a weak spirit, it should be able to read and search out the spirit's thought as well. How necessary, therefore, that the mind be kept in its normal state. Just as the movements of the spirit have their laws, so the activity of the mind is governed by its particular laws. The mind that can work freely is one which is light and lively. If it be expanded too far, like overstretching a bow, it shall sacrifice its effectiveness to work. The enemy well knows how we need our mind to attend the spirit so that we may walk by the spirit. Thus he frequently induces us to overuse it that it may be rendered unfit to function normally and hence be powerless to reinforce the spirit in time of weakness.

Our mind is much more than an organ of assistance to the spirit; it also is the place where we obtain light. The Spirit of God dispenses light to the mind through the spirit. If the mind is overexerted it relinquishes the power of receiving His light. The enemy understands that if our mind is darkened our whole being enters into darkness; he consequently strives with all his effort to provoke us to think so very much that we are unable to work quietly. To walk after the spirit a believer must inhibit his mind from revolving endlessly. If it turns too long around one topic, worries or grieves too much over matters, and ponders too intensively to know God's will, it may become unbearable and hamper its normal operation. The mind needs to be kept in a steady and secure state.

LESSON TWENTY-FIVE

THE NORMALCY OF THE SPIRIT

Blessed are the poor in spirit.

Matthew 5.3a

The Bible is not silent about the normalcy of a believer's spirit. Many matured ones have experienced what the Bible exhorts; they recognize that to retain their triumphant position and to cooperate with God they must preserve their spirit in the proper conditions laid down in the Word. We shall shortly see how it is to be controlled by the renewed will of the believer. This is a principle of great consequence, for by the will one is able to set his spirit in its proper place.

A CONTRITE SPIRIT

"Jehovah is nigh unto them that are of a broken heart, and saveth such as are of a contrite spirit" (Psalm 34.18 ASV).

"For thus says the high and lofty One who inhabits eternity, whose name is Holy: I dwell in the high and holy place, and also with him who is of a contrite and humble spirit" (Isaiah 57.15).

God's people often erroneously think that they need a contrite spirit only at the time they repent and believe in the Lord or whenever they subsequently fall into sin. We should know, however, that God wishes us to keep our spirit in a state of contrition at all times. Although we do not daily sin we are nonetheless required by Him to be of humble spirit constantly, because our flesh still exists and may be stirred up at any moment. Such contrition precludes our losing watchfulness. We ought never sin; yet we always should have sorrow for sin. The presence of God is felt in such a spirit.

A BROKEN SPIRIT

"The sacrifice acceptable to God is a broken spirit" (Psalm 51.17).

A broken spirit is one which trembles before God. Some Christians do not sense any uneasiness in their inner man after they have sinned. A healthy spirit will be broken before God—as was David's—upon once having sinned. It is not difficult to restore to God those who have a broken spirit.

A LOWLY SPIRIT

It is better to be of a lowly spirit with the poor than to divide the spoil with the proud. (Proverbs 16.19).

He who is lowly in spirit will obtain honor (Proverbs 29.23).

And also with him who is of a contrite and humble spirit, to revive the spirit of the humble (Isaiah 57.15).

Lowliness is not looking down on one's self; rather it is a not looking at one's self at all. As soon as a believer's spirit becomes haughty he is liable to fall. Humility is not only Godward but is manward as well. A lowly spirit is demonstrated when one associates with the poor. It is this spirit alone which does not despise any who are created by God. God's presence and glory is manifested in the life of the spiritually humble.

A FERVENT SPIRIT

"In diligence not slothful; fervent in spirit; serving the Lord" (Romans 12.11 ASV).

For a time the flesh may be fervent when it is emotionally excited, but this fervency does not endure. Even when the flesh seems most diligent it actually may be quite lazy, since it is diligent solely in those things with which it agrees; hence the flesh is impelled by emotion. It cannot serve God in matters which do not appeal to it nor when emotion is cold and low. It is impossible for the flesh to labor with the Lord in cloud as well as in sunshine, step by step, slowly but steadily. "Fervent in spirit" is a permanent feature; he therefore who possesses this spirit is qualified to serve the Lord endlessly. We should avoid all fervency of the flesh but allow the Holy Spirit to so fill our inner man that He may keep it perpetually fervent. Then our spirit will not turn cold when our emotion becomes chilled, nor will the work of the Lord collapse into a seemingly immovable state.

A JOYFUL SPIRIT

"My spirit rejoices in God my Savior" (Luke 1.47).

Towards himself a Christian should have a broken spirit (Psalm 51.17), but towards God it should be one of rejoicing always in Him. He rejoices not for its own sake nor because of any joyful experience, work, blessing or circumstance, but exclusively because God is his center. Indeed, no saint can genuinely rejoice out of any cause other than God Himself.

If our spirit is oppressed by worry, weight and sorrow it will commence to be irresponsible, next sink down, then lose its proper place, and finally become powerless to follow the leading of the Holy Spirit. When pressed down by a heavy load the spirit loses its lightness, freedom and brightness. It quickly topples from its ascendant position. And should the time of sorrow be prolonged, damage to spiritual life is incalculable. Nothing can save the situation except to rejoice in the Lord—rejoice in what God is and how He is our Savior. The note of hallelujah must never be in short supply in the spirit of the believer.

A HOLY SPIRIT

"To be holy in body and spirit" (1 Corinthians 7.34).

"Let us cleanse ourselves from every defilement of body and spirit" (2 Corinthians 7.1).

For anyone to walk in a spiritual manner it will be necessary for him to keep his spirit holy at all times. An unholy spirit leads people into error. Inordinate thought towards men or things, assessing the evil of others, a lack of love, loquacity (talkativeness), sharp criticism, self-righteousness, refusing entreaty (rejecting pleadings), jealousy, self-pride, and so forth—all these can defile the spirit. An unholy spirit cannot be fresh and new.

A STRONG SPIRIT

"Become strong in spirit" (Luke 1.80).

Our spirit is capable of growth and should increase gradually in strength. This is indispensable to spiritual life. How often we sense our spirit is not strong enough to control our soul and body, especially the moment the soul is stimulated or the body is weak. Sometimes in helping others we notice how heavily weighed down they are in their spirit, yet ours lacks the power to release them. Or when battling with the enemy we discover our spiritual strength is inadequate to wrestle long enough with the enemy until we win. Numberless are those occasions when we feel the spirit losing its grip; we have to force ourselves to proceed in life and in work. How we long for a more robust inner man!

As the spirit waxes stronger the power of intuition and discernment increases. We are fit to resist everything not of the spirit. Some who wish to walk after the spirit cannot because their inner man lacks the strength to control the soul and the body. We cannot expect the Holy Spirit to do anything for us; our regenerated spirit must instead cooperate with Him. We should learn how to *exercise* our spirit and use it to the limit of our understanding. Through exercise it will become progressively sturdier till it possesses the strength to eliminate all obstructions to the Holy Spirit; such hindrances as a stubborn will, a confused mind, or an undisciplined emotion.

THE BELIEVER AND EMOTION

You shall love the Lord your God with all your heart, and with all your soul, and with all your mind.

Matthew 22.37

Careful study of the soulish reveals that the conduct and action of such ones stem principally from their emotion. While the soul possesses three primary functions most soulish or carnal Christians belong to the emotional category. Their whole life appears to revolve largely around the impulses of emotion. In human affairs it seems to occupy a greater area than mind and will: it apparently plays a bigger role in daily life than do the other parts of the soul. Hence nearly all the practices of the soulish originate with emotion.

Our emotion emits joy, happiness, cheerfulness, excitement, elation, stimulation, despondency, sorrow, grief, melancholy, misery, moaning, dejection, confusion, anxiety, zeal, coldness, affection, aspiration, covetousness, compassion, kindness, preference, interest, expectation, pride, fear, remorse, hate, *et al.* The mind is the organ of our thinking and reasoning and the will, of our choices and decisions. Aside from our thought and intent and their related works, all other operations issue from emotion. Our thousand and one diverse feelings manifest its function. Feeling comprises such a vast area of our existence that most carnal Christians belong to the emotional type.

Man's sensational (sense) life is most comprehensive, hence highly complicated; to help believers understand it, we can gather all its various expressions into the three groups of (1) affection, (2) desire, and (3) feeling. These groups cover the three aspects of the function of emotion. Should a saint overcome all three, he is well on the way to entering upon a pure spiritual path.

To be sure, man's emotion is nothing but the manifold feelings he naturally has. He may be loving or hateful, joyful or sorrowful, excited or dejected, interested or uninterested, yet all are but the ways he feels. Should we take the trouble to observe ourselves we will easily perceive how changeful are our feelings. Few matters in the world are as changeable as emotion. We can be one way one minute and feel quite opposite the next. Emotion changes as feeling changes, and how rapidly the latter can change. He therefore who lives by emotion lives without principle.

Emotion may be denominated (considered as) the most formidable enemy to the life of a spiritual Christian. We know a child of God ought to walk by the spirit. To walk this way he needs to observe every direction given by his inner man. We know also, however, that these senses of the spirit are delicate as well as keen. Unless the child of God waits quietly and attentively to receive and discern the revelation in his intuition, he never can secure the guidance of his spirit. Consequently, the *total silence* of emotion is an indispensable condition to walking by the spirit. How often its small and delicate motion is disturbed and overpowered by the roaring of one's emotion. On no account can we attribute any fault to the smallness of the spirit's voice, for we have been endowed with the spiritual capacity to be able to hear it. No, it is entirely the mixing in of other voices that causes the Christian to miss the spirit's voice. But for that person who will maintain his emotion in silence, the voice of intuition can be detected easily.

The upsurge and decline of feeling may not only disqualify a believer from walking in the spirit but may also directly cause him to walk in the flesh. If he cannot follow the spirit he will naturally follow the flesh. Because he is unfit to obtain the guidance of his spirit, he invariably turns to his emotional impulse. Be it therefore recognized that when the spirit ceases to lead, emotion will do so. During such a period the believer will interpret emotional impulses to be motions of inspiration.

An emotional Christian can be compared to a pond of sand and mud: as long as no one disturbs the water the pond looks clear and clean; but let it be agitated a moment and its true muddy character appears.

INSPIRATION AND EMOTION

Many saints cannot distinguish inspiration from emotion. Actually these two can be defined readily. Emotion always enters from man's *outside*, whereas inspiration originates with the Holy Spirit in man's spirit. When a believer surveys the beauty of nature, he naturally senses a kind of feeling welling up within him. As he admires the fascinating landscape he is moved with pleasure. This is emotion. Or when he meets his loved one there surges through him an unspeakable feeling as though some sort of power is attracting him. This too is emotion. Both the beautiful scenery and the beloved one are outside the man—hence the stirrings aroused by these external elements belong to emotion. Inspiration, on the other hand, is quite the reverse. It is exclusively effected by the Holy Spirit *within* man. God's Spirit alone inspires; since He dwells in the human spirit, inspiration must come from within. Inspiration may be imparted in the coldest and most tranquil environment; it does not require the encouragement of scenic wonder or of dear ones. Emotion is just the opposite: it withers the instant outside help is removed. And so an emotional person thrives wholly in accordance with the particular environment of the given moment: with stimulation he can press on, without it he folds up. But inspiration needs no such outside aid; on the contrary, it becomes confused should emotion be unduly influenced by external environment.

The Lord's people should be cautious, however, lest they view coldness and absence of constraint to be barometers of spirituality. Such an assumption is far from the truth. Know we not that the mark of emotion is dejection as well as excitation? Know we not that emotion cools as well as stirs? When emotion arouses a man he is elated, but when it mollifies him (emotion cools down) he feels depressed. Driven by high emotion, the Christian commits many errors. Upon awakening to this fact, however, he tends to suppress his feelings altogether. And so now he conceives himself as spiritual. Yet what he does not realize is that this is but a reactionary impulse of that self-same *emotion* of his which has calmed him down; that following a time of excitement, there is bound to emerge an emotional *re*-action. Such coldness and dullness precipitates the believer to lose interest in God's work: it deprives him as well his brotherly affection towards God's children. Because of the reluctance of the outer man to work, the believer's inner man is imprisoned and the life of the spirit is powerless to flow out. Now during this episode the saint may deem himself to be walking after the spirit, for, he reasons within himself, am I not today an extremely cold person and no longer burning wildly as before? Little does this Christian comprehend that he continues to walk after emotion anyway, only this time after the other extreme of emotion!

Today men give much attention to psychology. Even many who serve the Lord feel they *must* diligently study psychology. These believe if only their words, teachings, presentations, manners and interpretations can be made psychologically appealing to people, that many could be won to Christ. Psychology naturally refers in large part to the workings of man's emotion. Occasionally it does seem to be helpful, but a child of God who relies on emotion serves no productive purpose for the Lord.

THE PROPER USE OF EMOTION

If God's children permit the cross to operate deeply upon their emotion they shall find afterwards that it no longer obstructs, but rather cooperates with, their spirit. The cross has dealt with the natural life in the emotion, has renewed it, and has made it a channel for the spirit. A spiritual man we have said before is not a spirit, but neither is he a person devoid of emotion; on the contrary, the spiritual man will use his feeling to express the divine life in him. Before it is touched by God, emotion follows its own whim. And hence it habitually fails to be an instrument of the spirit. But once it is purified it can serve as the means of the spirit's expression. The inner man needs emotion to express its life: it needs emotion to declare its love and its sympathy towards man's suffering: and it also needs emotion to make man sense the movement of its intuition. Spiritual sensing is usually made known through the feeling of a quiet and pliable emotion. If emotion is pliably subject to the spirit the latter, through the emotion, will love or hate exactly as God wishes.

Some Christians, upon discerning the truth of not living by feeling, mistake spiritual life as one without it. They accordingly try to destroy it and to render themselves as insensate as wood and stone. Because of their ignorance of the meaning of the death of the cross, they do not understand what is meant by handing over one's emotion to death and living by the spirit. We do not say that, in order to be spiritual, a Christian must become exceedingly hard and void of affection like inanimate objects—as though the term spiritual man means for him to be emptied of feeling. Quite the contrary. The most tender, merciful, loving, and sympathetic of persons is a spiritual man. To be entirely spiritual by delivering his emotion to the cross does not denote that henceforth he is stripped of his feeling. We have observed numerous spiritual saints and have noticed that their love is greater than that of others, which demonstrates that a spiritual man is not without emotion and additionally that it differs from that of the ordinary man.

LESSON TWENTY-SEVEN

AFFECTION

As the deer pants for the water brooks, so my soul pants for You, O God.

Psalm 42.1 (NASV)

Yielding one's affection to the Lord may be viewed by the Christian to be a most difficult task, yet the Lord is concerned with one's affection more than with any other matter. He demands him to present his affection wholly to Him and let Him lord over it. The Lord asks for first place in our affection. We often hear people talk about consecration, but this act is simply the first step in one's spiritual walk. Consecration is not the destination of spirituality, it is but its beginning. It leads a Christian to a sanctified position. In a word, without consecration there can be no spiritual life. Even so, nothing is more paramount in one's consecration than is his affection. Whether or not this has been yielded determines the truth or falsity of consecration. Its acid test is affection. Relatively easy is it for us to hand over our time, money, power, and countless other items; but to offer our affection is exceedingly difficult. This is not to imply we do not love Christ; perhaps we love our Lord very much. Nevertheless, if we grant first place in our affection to another and relegate Christ to second place, or if we love someone else while loving the Lord, or if we ourselves direct our affection, then what we have offered is not considered consecration for we have not yielded our affection. Every spiritual believer appreciates the necessity for affection to be offered first. For without that, nothing really is offered.

God the Father demands absolute love from His children. He is unwilling to share our heart with anyone or anything else: even if He should receive the bigger share, He is still not pleased. God demands all our love. Naturally this strikes a fatal blow to one's soul life. The Lord bids us part with what we ourselves cling to, for it divides our heart. He asks us to love Him totally and to utterly follow Him in love: "You shall love the Lord your God with all your heart, and with all your soul, and with all your mind" (Matthew 22.37). "All" denotes every ounce of it for the Lord. He enjoins us to reserve not one tiny particle of affection which we ourselves can direct. He calls for all. He is a jealous God (Exodus 20.5), therefore He does not allow anybody to steal the love of His children.

We cannot but stress the significance of our loving the Lord with our whole heart. Nothing satisfies His heart as does our love. The Lord looks not for our laboring for Him but for our loving Him. The church at Ephesus, according to Revelation 2, works and toils for the Lord, yet He is displeased with them because they have abandoned their first love. If our service is rendered for love's sake the Lord will certainly be pleased; but what value is it to Him if we undertake endeavors for Him without truly possessing a heart for Him? We should be aware how possible it is to labor for the Lord and yet not love the Lord. Let us ask God to cast light on the reason for our activity. Is love for the Lord strong within us? What is the use of calling out "Lord, Lord" and working diligently for Him while simultaneously the heart has no love for Him? May we have a perfect heart towards our dearly beloved Lord!

Actually, only God can satisfy a Christian's heart; man cannot. The failure of many is to seek from man what can be found only in God. All human affection is empty; the love of God alone is able to fully satisfy one's desire. The moment a Christian seeks a love outside God his spiritual life immediately falls. We can only live by the love of God.

What then? Does this indicate we need not love man? The Bible repeatedly charges us to love the brethren and even to love our enemies. Accordingly we know it is not God's will we should not love man, but He does desire to *manage* our affection towards all men. God does not want us to love others for our sake but to love for His sake and in Him. Our natural

145

likes and dislikes do not have any part here; natural affection must lose its power. God wants us, for love's sake, to accept His control. When He wishes us to love someone, we instantly are able to; should He also desire us to terminate our relationship with someone, we can do that too.

This is the pathway of the cross. Only as we allow it to cut deeply so that we have our soul life delivered to death can we be rid of self in our affections. If we genuinely have undergone death we will not be *attached* to anyone but will be guided solely by the command of God. Our soul life, as it experiences death, loses its power and becomes as much as dead in the matter of affection. God will then direct us how in Him to renew our love for men. God wants us to create in Him a new relationship with those we formerly loved. Every natural relationship has been terminated. New relationships are established through death and resurrection.

LOVING THE LORD SOULISHLY

Right here we should sound a note of warning. Never think we ourselves can love the Lord. Whatever comes from us is rejected by Him; even loving Him is unacceptable. On the one hand, the believer's lack of deep affection towards the Lord grieves Him greatly; on the other hand, one's loving Him with *soul power* is not welcomed by God either. Our affection, even when used to love the Lord, must be entirely under the spirit's management. Too many love the Lord with a worldly love and too few, with God's pure love.

What, therefore, is the distinction between spiritual love and soulish love towards God? These two are not readily distinguishable outwardly, but inwardly every Christian can detect the true source of his love. As the soul is our very self so all which belongs to it cannot draw away from self. A soulish affection is one in which self is working. To love God for the sake of personal pleasure is carnal love. If a love is spiritual it has no self mixed in with loving God. It means to love God for His Own sake. Any affection which is totally or partially for one's own pleasure or for reasons other than for God Himself emanates from the soul.

Another way we can distinguish the source of love is through its results. If one's love is soulical it does not empower him to be delivered permanently from the world. The believer must continue to worry and struggle to break away from the world's attraction. Not so with spiritual love. Here the things of the world just naturally fade away before it. The one who participates in that kind of love despises the world, considering its things abhorrent and abominable. Henceforth he appears to be unable to see the world because the glory of God has blinded his physical eyes. Furthermore, a person who experiences such love as this becomes humble as though he has dried up before men.

The nature of God's love is unchangeable. Ours alternates all too readily. If it is our habit to love God with our own affection we shall turn cold towards Him whenever we are unhappy. We shall lose our own love should we have to go through a long period of trial. Our affection towards God will recede when we cannot obtain the pleasure we expect, because we love Him with our own love and for our own sake. If it were God's love it would remain in the condition of loving Him through every circumstance. "For love is strong as death, jealousy is cruel as the grave . . . Many waters cannot quench love, neither can floods drown it" (Song of Solomon 8.6-7). The believer who genuinely loves God will persist in loving Him regardless what he encounters or how he feels. A soulical affection ceases when the movement of emotion ceases; but a spiritual affection is strong, ever unrelenting, for it never relinquishes.

LESSON TWENTY-EIGHT

DESIRE

Whom have I in heaven but Thee? And there is nothing upon earth that I desire besides Thee.

Psalm 73.25

Desire occupies the largest part of our emotional life: it joins forces with our will to rebel against God's will. Our innumerable desires create such confused feelings in us that we cannot quietly follow the spirit. They arouse our feelings and make for many turbulent experiences. Before one is set free from the power of sin his desire unites with sin in making him love sin and in depriving the new man of his freedom. After he is liberated from sin's outward manifestations the same desire drives him to seek for *himself* many things outside of God. And while a person is still in the emotional state he is controlled mainly by his desire. Not until the cross has performed its deeper work and one's desire has been judged in the light of the cross can he wholly live in the spirit and for God.

When a Christian remains carnal he is ruled vigorously by his desire. All natural or soulish desires and ambitions are linked with *self* life. They are for self, by self, or after self. While carnal, one's will is not yielded fully to the Lord, and so he holds many ideas of his own. His desire then works together with his ideas to make him delight in what he wills to have and to expect to have his own ideas realized. All self-delight, self-glory, self-exaltation, self-love, self-pity and self-importance issue from man's desire and render self the center of everything. Can we conjure up anything man himself desires which is not linked to something of self? If we examine ourselves in the light of the Lord we shall see that all our aspirations, no matter how noble, cannot escape the bounds of self. All are for it! If they are not self-pleasing, then they

148

are self-glorifying. How can a Christian live in the spirit if he is engulfed in such a condition?

Pride springs from desire. Man aspires to obtain a place for himself that he may feel honored before men. All secret boastings about one's position, family, health, temperament, ability, good looks, and power flow from man's natural desire. To dwell on how differently one lives, dresses and eats and to feel self-content in these differences is also the work of emotion. Even to esteem the gift one receives from God as superior to that of others is inspired by natural desire as well.

How extensively an emotional believer comes to display himself! He loves both to see and to be seen. He cannot abide the restraints of God. He will try every means to push himself to the front. He is unable to be hidden according to the will of God and to deny himself when he is hidden. He wishes others to notice him. When he is not duly respected his desire of self-love suffers a deep wound. But if he is admired by people his heart is overjoyed. He loves to hear praising voices and considers them just and true. He also attempts to elevate himself in his work, whether in preaching or in writing, for his secret self motive goads him on. In a word, this one has not yet died to his desire of vainglory. He is still seeking what *he* desires and what can inflate *him*.

The more a person is spiritual the more real he becomes, for he has been united with God and is at rest. But when one is goaded by his natural life he becomes very pretentious. He carries a reckless spirit and likes to do daring things in order to satisfy himself and impress others. How he pretends to be mature and wise when actually he is immature in many of his undertakings. He may regret his pretension afterwards but for the moment he feels great. Anyone who pursues such desires cannot avoid going off on a tangent.

Desire for haste is another symptom of the emotional Christian. One who moves by his natural feeling does not know how to wait on God nor is he acquainted with the leading of the Holy Spirit. Emotion is usually hasty. A Christian emotionally excited acts hastily. It is extremely hard for him to wait on the Lord, to know the will of God, and to walk step by step in that will. Indeed, the Lord's people are incapable of following the spirit unless their emotion is truly yielded to the cross. Let us remember that out of a hundred impulsive actions scarcely one is in the will of God.

Self-justification is a common symptom among emotional Christians. The Lord's people often encounter misunderstandings. Sometimes He enjoins them to explain their situations; but unless one is so instructed by the Lord, his explanations are but the agitations of his soul life. More often than not the Lord wishes His people to commit all matters into His hand and not defend themselves. How we like to speak on our own behalf! How awful for us to be misunderstood! It diminishes one's glory and deflates one's self-esteem. The self in man cannot remain silent when an unjustified fault is leveled at him. He cannot accept what is given him by God nor can he stay for God to justify him. He believes God's justification will come too late; he demands the Lord to justify him at once so that everybody may behold his righteousness in no uncertain terms. All this is but the ferment of soulish desire. Were the believer willing to humble himself beneath the mighty hand of God at the instance of misunderstanding, he would discover that God wishes to use this occasion to equip him to deny his self more deeply; that is, to deny once again his soulish desire. This constitutes the Christian's practical cross. Each time he accepts a cross he experiences once more its crucifixion. Should he follow his natural concern and rush to defend himself, he shall find the power of self more formidable to subdue on the next occasion.

If anyone wishes to maintain a true spiritual course he must cooperate with God in putting to death his own desire. All interests, inclinations and preferences must be denied. We should gladly accept man's contradicting, despising, discounting, misunderstanding, and harsh criticising and permit these matters which are so antagonistic to natural desire to deal with our soul life. We should learn how to receive suffering, pain, or a lowly place as apportioned us by God. However much our self life feels pained or our natural feeling is hurt, we must bear them patiently. If we bear the cross in practical matters we shall shortly see our self life crucified on the cross we bear. For to carry the cross is to be crucified thereon. Every time we silently accept what goes against our natural disposition we receive another nail which pins our soul life more firmly to the cross. All vainglory has to die. Our longing to be seen, respected, worshiped, exalted and proclaimed needs to be crucified. Any heart for self-display must equally be crucified. Every pretension to spirituality in order to be praised must be cut down; so must all self-importance and self-exaltation. Our desire, whatever its expression, must be denied. Anything which is initiated by ourselves is defiled in the sight of God.

The practical cross which God dispenses runs counter to our desires. The cross aims at crucifying them. Nothing in our total make-up suffers more wounding under the lash of the cross than does our emotion. It cuts deeply into everything pertaining to ourselves. How then can our emotion be happy when our desire is dying? The redemption of God requires a thorough setting aside of the old creation. God's will and our soul's delight are incompatible. For anyone to pursue the Lord he must oppose his own desire.

Once he loses his heart for "self" the believer can be wholly God's. He is ready to be molded into any form God wishes. His desire no longer strives against God; nay, he relishes nothing but God. His life has now become quite simple: he has no expectations, no requests, no ambitions other than to be willingly obedient to the Lord's will. A life of obedience to His intent is the simplest kind on earth, because he who so lives seeks nothing but to quietly follow God.

The Lord Jesus speaks to His disciples saying: "Take my yoke upon you, and learn from me; for I am gentle and lowly in heart, and you will find rest for your souls" (Matthew 11.29). The soul here alludes especially to the emotional part of our being. The Lord knows that His Own people must pass through many trials, that the heavenly Father is going to arrange for them to be lonely and misunderstood. As no one understands Him except the Father, so no one will understand His disciples (v.27). Jesus knows that the heavenly Father must permit many unpleasant occurrences to befall the believers in order that they may be weaned from the world. He also appreciates what the feelings in their souls will be like as they are put through the fire. For this reason He tells them in advance to learn from Him so that they may find rest for their emotion. Jesus is gentle: He is able to receive any treatment from men: He joyfully accepts the opposition of sinners. Jesus is likewise lowly: He heartily humbles Himself: He has no ambition of His Own. The ambitious are hurt, angry, and restless when they cannot obtain their wishes. But Christ at all times lives gently and humbly on earth; there is consequently no occasion for His emotion to boil and erupt. He teaches that we should learn from Him, that we should be gentle and lowly as He is. He says for us to bear His yoke as a restraint upon ourselves. He bears a yoke too, even the yoke of God. He is satisfied with His Father's will alone; as long as the Father knows and understands Him, why should He be concerned about the opposition of others? He is willing to accept the restrictions given him by God. He explains that we must bear His yoke, accept His restraint, do His will, and seek no freedom for the flesh. If this is done, then nothing can disturb or provoke our emotion. This is the cross. If anyone is willing to receive the cross of Christ and submit completely to the Lord, he shall find rest for his emotion.

This is none other than a *satisfied life*. The Christian cherishes nothing but God; henceforth he is satisfied with His will. God himself has filled his desire. He regards everything God has arranged or given, asked or charged him with, as good. If he can but follow the will of God his heart is satisfied. He seeks his own pleasure no longer, and not because of force but because God's will has satisfied him. Since he is now filled, he has no more requests to make. A life such as this can be summed up in one word: satisfied. The characteristic of spiritual life is satisfaction—not in the sense of self-centeredness, self-sufficiency, or self-filling but in that of the person having found all his needs fully met in God. To him God's will is the very best; he is satisfied. What else need he ask for? Only emotional Christians find fault with God's arrangement and aspire to have more by conceiving numberless expectations in their hearts. But one who has allowed the Holy Spirit to operate deeply in him by the cross no longer yearns for anything according to himself. His desire is fulfilled already in God.

LESSON TWENTY-NINE

A LIFE OF FEELING

For we walk by faith, not by sight.

2 Corinthians 5.7 (NASV)

When Christians become affectionately attached to the Lord they are usually experiencing a life of feeling. Such an experience for them is most precious. They enter this phase of their Christian walk generally following their emancipation from sin and before their entrance upon a true spiritual life. Because they lack spiritual knowledge, these Christians often assume this kind of emotional experience to be most spiritual and most heavenly since it is encountered primarily after release from sin and affords them great pleasure. The delight it bestows is so satisfactory that they find it difficult to cut loose and forsake it.

During this period the believer senses the nearness of the Lord, so near that the hands can almost touch Him. He is alive to the delicate sweetness of the Lord's love as well as gripped by his own intense love towards the Lord. A fire seems to be burning in his heart; it leaves him with an unspeakable joy which makes him feel he is already in heaven. Something is heaving in his bosom, yielding indescribable pleasure, as though he were in possession of a priceless treasure. This sensation continues with him as he walks and works. Whenever the believer passes through this type of experience he wonders where his abode is, for he seems to have shed his earthly tent and now soars away with the angels.

For the moment Bible reading becomes a real delight. The more he reads the more joyous he feels. Prayer is also very easy. How wonderful to pour out his heart to God. The more he communes the brighter the heavenly light shines. He is able to make many decisions before the Lord which indicates how much he loves Him. Great is his longing to be quiet and alone with God; if only he could close his door forever and commune with the Lord his joy would be full, for no tongue can speak nor pen can write of the joy that lies therein. Formerly he was gregarious, as though crowds and individuals could satisfy his needs; but today he cherishes solitude because what he could derive from the crowds can never be compared to the joy he now receives when alone with his Lord. He favors seclusion more than companionship for fear that among men he may lose his joy.

Moreover, service assumes considerable spontaneity. Hitherto he appeared to have nothing to say, but now with the fire of love aglow in his heart he experiences multiplied pleasure in telling others of the Lord. The more he speaks the more anxious he is to speak. To suffer for the Lord becomes sweet to him. Since he senses Him so near and dear, he gladly embraces the thought of martyrdom. All burdens turn light and all hardships grow easy.

According to the believer's interpretation, he is at his spiritual peak when in possession of the wonderful feeling: he is at his lowest when deprived of it. He often characterizes his walk as full of ups and downs. By this he means that while he is feeling joyful, loving the Lord and sensing His presence he is at his spiritual best; but if his inward sensation is marked by dryness and pain he must be at his spiritual worst. In other words, he is spiritual so long as the warm fire of love is burning in his heart but soulish if his heart turns icy cold. Such is the common notion among Christians. Is it accurate? It is totally inaccurate. Unless we understand how it is wrong we shall suffer defeat to the very end.

A Christian should recognize that "feeling" is exclusively a part of the soul. When he lives by sensation, no matter what the kind, he is being soulish. During the period that he feels joyful, is loving the Lord and senses His presence, he is walking by feeling; likewise, during the period that he feels just the opposite he is *still* walking by feeling. Just as he is soulish whose life and labor are dictated by a refreshing, bright and joyous sensation, so is he equally soulish whose walk and work are determined by a dry, gloomy and painful one. A real spiritual life is never dominated by, nor lived in, feeling. Rather does it regulate feeling. Nowadays Christians mistake a life of feeling for spiritual experience. This is because many have never entered into genuine spirituality and hence interpret happy sensation to be spiritual experience. They do not know that such feeling is still soulical. Only what occurs in the intuition is spiritual experience—the rest is merely soulical activity.

THE AIMS OF GOD

Why then does God impart and later withdraw these feelings? Because He has a number of aims He wishes to fulfill.

First. God grants joy to believers to draw them closer to Him. He uses His gifts to attract men to Himself. He expects His children to believe in His love in every circumstance after He has once shown how gracious and loving He is towards them. Unfortunately Christians love God only when they sense His love and forget Him the moment they do not.

Second. God deals with our lives in this fashion in order to help us understand ourselves. We realize the hardest lesson to learn is that of knowing oneself—to appreciate how corrupt, empty, sinful, and void of good one is. This lesson has to be absorbed *throughout life.* The deeper one learns it the more one perceives the depth of uncleanness of his life and nature in the eyes of the Lord. Yet this is instruction which we do not relish learning nor is our natural life able to learn it. Hence the Lord employs many ways to teach and to lead us into this knowledge of self. Among His numerous ways the most important is this giving of joyous feeling and later taking it away. Through such treatment one begins to comprehend his corruptness. In the state of aridity he may come to see how in the former days of joy he misused God's gift in uplifting himself and despising others, and how he many times acted through the ferment of emotion rather than with the spirit. Such realization evokes humility. Had he understood that this experience is arranged by God to assist him to know himself, he would not have sought blissful sensation so intently as though it were the summit. God desires us to recognize that we may act just as often in dishonoring God's name when in ecstasy as when in anguish. We progress no more during the bright than during the dull period. Our life is equally corrupt in either condition.

Third. God aims to help His children overcome their environment. A Christian should not allow his surroundings to change his life. He whose path is altered by the influence of environment is not deeply experienced in the Lord. We have learned already that what can be affected by environment is emotion. It is when our emotion is influenced by environment that our lives undergo change. How imperative therefore for us to conquer emotion if we wish to overcome environment. To conquer his surroundings the Christian must prevail over all his various sensations. If he cannot surmount his ever vacillating feeling how can he overcome his environment? It is our feeling which is alive to any shift in environment and which varies accordingly. If we do not override our sensation our lives shall oscillate with our changing sensation. Thus do we need to overcome feeling before we can overcome environment.

This explains why the Lord leads one through different feelings in order that he may learn how to quell these feelings and thereby triumph over his surroundings. If he can subdue his strong and contrasting sensations he surely will be able to cope with the changing atmosphere. Thus will he achieve a steadfast and established walk, no longer drifting with the tide. God desires His child to remain the same with or without high feeling. He wants His child to commune with Him and serve

Him faithfully whether he is happy or is sad. God's child must not reshape his life according to how he feels. If he is serving the Lord faithfully and making intercession for others, then he should do so in gladness or in sorrow. He should not serve only when he feels refreshed and cease serving when he is parched. If we cannot subdue our many varied sensations then we can in no wise conquer our diverse surroundings. He who fails to surmount his environment is one who has failed to subjugate his feeling.

Fourth. God has another objective in view. He purposes to train our will. A genuine spiritual life is not one of feeling; rather, it is a life of will. The volition of a spiritual man has been renewed already by the Holy Spirit: it now awaits the spirit's revelation before it issues a command to the whole being. Unfortunately the will of quite a few saints is often so weak that either it cannot carry through the commands given it or, under the influence of emotion, it rejects God's will. To train and strengthen the will consequently becomes a very essential step.

Fifth. Via such leading God longs to guide the Christian onto a higher level of existence. If we carefully examine the Christian's walk we shall realize that the Lord at each instance He has desired to lead His own to a higher spiritual plateau first gave that one a taste of such a life in his feeling. We may say that on every occasion that one experiences a life of feeling, he has reached one more station on his spiritual journey. God grants him a foretaste of what He desires him to have: first He arranges for the Christian to sense it and next He withdraws the sensation so that by his spirit through his will he may keep what he has felt. If his spirit can press on with the assistance of his will, the Christian, by disregarding his emotion, can then see that he has made real progress in his walk. This is confirmed by our common experience. While we are pursuing an up-and-down type of existence we usually assume we have not made any advance. We conclude that during these months or years we have simply gone forward and then backward or simply backwards and then forwards. If, however, we were to compare our current spiritual state with that which obtained at the *commencement* of such alternating phenomena, we would discover we have actually *made some progress.* We advance unknowingly.

THE DANGER OF THIS LIFE

There is positively no danger if, while having such an experience, we comprehend its meaning and press forward in accordance with God's will. But it can be highly hazardous to spiritual life if we do not apprehend God's will and fail to resist our living by feeling; that is, when we encounter a buoyant feeling we advance unhesitatingly, but in the absence of such sensation we refuse to move at all. Those who make feeling their principle of life expose themselves to many dangers.

Anyone who walks by blissful emotions is usually weak in his will. It is unable to follow the direction of the spirit. The development of spiritual sensing is hampered by substituting his feeling for the spirit's intuition. He walks by his emotion. His intuition on the one side is suppressed by emotion and on the other is left unused; it is barely growing. Now intuition is active solely when emotion is quiet; only then can it communicate its thought to man. It waxes strong if it is often exercised. But the will of that person who leans on feeling is deprived of its sovereign power: his intuition is stifled and cannot transmit a distinct voice. Since the will thereby slips into a withered condition, the believer requires even more *help from feeling* to provoke the will to work. The will turns by feeling. If the latter is high the will is active; but should it be taken away the will suspends action. It is powerless to do anything by itself; it relies on the activation of emotion to propel it. Meanwhile the believer's spiritual life naturally sinks lower and lower until it seems that whenever emotion is absent no spiritual life is indicated at all. The operation of emotion has become an opiate to such ones! How tragic that some remain unconscious of this fact and seek emotion as the zenith of spiritual life.

Another danger may arise for those who live by sensation rather than by the spirit through the will: they may be deceived by Satan. This is one matter about which we ought to inform ourselves. Satan is skillful in counterfeiting the feelings which come from God. If with diverse kinds of sensations he attempts to confuse Christians who aspire to walk wholly after the spirit, how much more will he play his tricks on those who desire to follow their feeling. In their pursuit of emotion they fall directly into the hand of Satan, for he delights to supply them with all kinds of feeling which they assume to be from God.

THE LIFE OF FAITH

The righteous shall live by faith.

Romans 1.17

The Bible discloses for us the normal path of a Christian's walk in such passages as "the righteous shall live by faith"; "the life I now live in the flesh I live by faith in the Son of God"; and "we walk by faith, not by sight" (Romans 1.17 ASV; Galatians 2.20; 2 Corinthians 5.7). By faith are we to live. But while this principle may be quickly grasped in the mind it is not so readily experienced in life.

The life of faith is not only totally different from, but also diametrically opposite to, a life of feeling. He who lives by sensation can follow God's will or seek the things above purely at the time of excitement; should his blissful feeling cease, every activity terminates. Not so with one who walks by faith. Faith is anchored in the One Whom he believes rather than in the one who exercises the believing, that is, himself. Faith looks not at what happens to him but at Him Whom he believes. Though he may completely change, yet the One in Whom he trusts never does—and so he can proceed without letting up. Faith establishes its relationship with God. It regards not its feeling because it is concerned with God. Faith follows the One believed while feeling turns on how one feels. What faith thus beholds is God whereas what feeling beholds is one's self. God does not change: He is the same God in either the cloudy day or the sunny day. Hence he who lives by faith is as unchanging as is God; he expresses the same kind of life through darkness or through light. But one who dwells by feeling must pursue an up-and-down existence because his feeling is ever changing.

The Christian experience, from start to finish, is a journey of faith. Through it we come into possession of a new life and through it we walk by this new life. Faith is the life principle of a Christian. This is of course acknowledged by all saints; but strangely enough many seem to overlook this in their experience. They forget that to live and to move by emotion or happy sensations is to do so by sight and not by faith What is the life of faith? It is one lived contrary to a life of feeling because it disregards feeling altogether. If Christians desire to live by this principle they should not alter their demeanor or bitterly cry as though bereft of their spiritual life whenever they feel cold, dry, empty, or pained. We live by faith and not by joy.

We should inquire once again as to what the life of faith is. It is one lived by believing God *under any circumstance*: "If he slay me," says Job, "yet would I trust in Him" (13.15 Darby). That is faith. Because I once believed, loved and trusted God I shall believe, love and trust Him wherever He may put me and however my heart and body may suffer. Nowadays the people of God expect to feel peaceful even in the time of physical pain. Who is there who dares to renounce this consolation of heart for the sake of believing God? Who is there who can accept God's will joyfully and continuously commit himself to Him even though he *feels* that God hates him and desires to slay him? That is the highest life. Of course God would never treat us like that. Nevertheless in the walk of the most advanced Christians they seem to experience something of this apparent desertion by God. Would we be able to remain unmoved in our faith in God if we felt thus? Observe what John Bunyan, author of *Pilgrim's Progress*, proclaimed when men sought to hang him: "If God does not intervene I shall leap into eternity with blind faith come heaven, come hell!" There was a hero of faith! In the hour of despair can we too say, "O God, though You desert me yet will I believe You"? Emotion begins to doubt when it senses blackness, whereas faith holds on to God even in the face of death.

THE LIFE OF THE WILL

The life of faith can be called the life of the will since faith is impervious to how one feels but chooses through volition to obey God's mind. Though the Christian may not *feel* like obeying God, even so he *wills* to obey Him. We find two opposite kinds of Christians: one depends on emotion, the other relies on the *renewed* will. A Christian who trusts in feeling can obey God solely while he is deriving stimulus from his feeling, that is, excitable feeling. The one however who depends on volition determines that he shall serve God amid whatever circumstance or feeling. His will reflects his real opinion whereas his feeling is only activated by outside stimulus. From God's viewpoint not much value accrues in doing His will out of a pleasurable sensation: to do so is merely to be persuaded by the joy of God and not by a wholehearted aspiration to do His will. Except he neither feels a bit of joy nor is stimulated by some wonderful feeling and yet decides to do God's will can the Christian's obedience be counted truly valuable, because it flows from his honest heart and expresses his respect for God and disregard of self. The distinction between the spiritual and the soulish Christian lies precisely there: the soulish primarily considers himself and therefore only obeys God when he feels his desire is satisfied; the spiritual has a will fully cooperating with God and hence accepts His arrangement without wavering even though he has no outside help or stimulus.

After a believer has thus been dealt with, he can commence the walk of faith which is true spiritual life. And the one who arrives at this position enters upon a life of rest. The fire of the cross has consumed his every greedy pursuit. He at last has learned his lesson: he recognizes that God's will alone is precious. All else, though naturally desirable, is incompatible with the highest life of God. Now he rejoices in relinquishing everything. Whatever the Lord deems necessary to withdraw,

163

he gladly allows His hand to do it. The sighing, mourning and grieving which arose out of his former anticipation, seeking and struggling have today entirely disappeared. He realizes that the loftiest life is one lived for God and one obedient to His will. Though he has lost everything yet is he satisfied with the fulfillment of God's purpose. Though he is left with nothing to enjoy, yet is he humble under the ordering of God. So long as the Lord is pleased he cares not the least what happens to him. He now has perfect rest; nothing external can any longer stimulate him.

Upon arriving at this restful position the believer shall find that all he heretofore had lost for the Lord's sake has today been restored. He has gained God, and therefore everything belonging to God belongs to him as well. What the Lord had withdrawn before he now can properly enjoy in Him. The reason why God at the beginning had led him through many sorrows was because his soul life lay behind everything, seeking and asking too much for *himself*, desiring even things which were outside God's will. Such independent action had to be circumscribed by God. Now that he has lost himself— that is, his natural life—the Christian is in a position to enjoy the bliss of God within its legitimate boundary. Not till today was he qualified to be rightly related to His joy. Hereafter he can thankfully accept whatever is given him, because the eagerness to secure something for self has already been put to nought; he does not petition inordinately for that which was not bestowed upon him.

LESSON THIRTY-ONE

THE MIND A BATTLEFIELD

We destroy arguments and every proud obstacle to the knowledge of God and take every thought captive to obey Christ.

2 Corinthians 10.5

The mind of man is his organ of thought. Through it he is equipped to know, think, imagine, remember, and understand. Man's intellect, reasoning, wisdom and cleverness all pertain to the mind. Broadly speaking the mind is the brain. Mind is a psychological term whereas brain is a physiological term. The mind of psychology is the brain of physiology. Man's mind occupies a large place in his life because his thought easily influences his action.

Before Regeneration

According to the Bible the mind of man is unusual in that it constitutes a battlefield where Satan and his evil spirits contend against the truth and hence against the believer. We may illustrate as follows. Man's will and spirit are like a citadel which the evil spirits crave to capture. The open field where the battle is waged for the seizure of the citadel is man's mind. Note how Paul the Apostle describes it: "though we live in the world we are not carrying on a worldly war, for the weapons of our warfare are not worldly but have divine power to destroy strongholds. We destroy *arguments* and every proud obstacle to the knowledge of God, and take every *thought* captive to obey Christ" (2 Corinthians 10.3-5). He initially tells us of a battle—then where the battle is fought—and finally for what objective. This struggle pertains exclusively to man's mind. The Apostle likens man's arguments or reasonings to an enemy's strongholds. He pictures the mind as held by the enemy; it must therefore be broken into by waging war. He concludes that many rebellious thoughts are housed in these strongholds and need to be taken captive to the obedience of Christ. All this plainly shows us that the mind of man is the scene of battle where the evil spirits clash with God.

Scripture explains that before regeneration "the god of this world (had) blinded the minds of the unbelievers, to keep them from seeing the light of the gospel of the glory of Christ, who is the likeness of God" (2 Corinthians 4.4). This verse concurs in what the other verse just quoted said by declaring here that Satan holds on to man's mind by making it blind. Some people perhaps may consider themselves extremely wise in their ability to advance many arguments against the gospel; others may take for granted that unbelief is due to dullness of understanding; but the truth in both cases is that the eyes of man's mind have been covered by Satan. When firmly held by Satan the mind of man becomes "hardened"; man "follows the desires of body and mind (as) children of wrath" and so "is estranged and hostile in mind" because "the mind that is set on the flesh is hostile to God" (2 Corinthians 3.14; Ephesians 2.3; Colossians 1.21; Romans 8.7).

Prior to regeneration man's intellect obstructs him from apprehending God. It is necessary for His mighty power to destroy man's arguments. This is a work which must occur at the hour of new birth—and it does happen then in the form of repentance. The original definition of repentance is none else than "a change of mind." Man in his mind is at enmity with God; therefore God must alter man's mind if He would impart life to him. In his unregenerated state man has a darkened mind; at his regeneration it undergoes a drastic change. Because it has been so united with the devil it is vital for man to receive from God a change of mind before he can receive a new heart (Acts 11.18).

AFTER REGENERATION

But even following repentance the believer's mind is not liberated totally from the touch of Satan. As the enemy worked through the mind in former days, so today will he work in the same manner. Paul, in writing to the Corinthian *believers*, confided that he was "afraid that as the serpent deceived Eve by his cunning, your *thoughts* will be led astray from a sincere and pure devotion to Christ" (2 Corinthians 11. 3). The Apostle well recognizes that as the god of this world blinds the mind of unbelievers so will he deceive the mind of the believers. Even though they are saved their life of thought is as yet unrenewed; consequently it remains the most strategic battleground. *The mind suffers the onslaughts of the powers of darkness more than any other organ of the whole man.* We should realize that satanic spirits are directing special attention to our minds and are attacking them unrelentingly—"as the serpent deceived Eve by his cunning." Satan did not assail Eve's heart first but rather her head. Similarly today, the evil spirits first attack our head, not our heart, in order to have us corrupted from the simplicity and purity which is towards Christ. They fully understand how it is the *weakest* point in our entire being, for it had served as their fortress before we believed and even now is not yet entirely overthrown. Attacking the mind is the easiest avenue for them to accomplish their purpose. Eve's heart was sinless and yet she received Satan's suggested thoughts. She was thus beguiled through his deception into forfeiting her reasoning and tumbling into the snare of the enemy. Let a believer accordingly be careful in his boast of possessing an honest and sincere heart, for unless he learns how to repulse the evil spirits in his mind he will continue to be tempted and deceived into losing the sovereignty of his will.

It is possible for a child of God to have a new life and a

new heart but be without a new head. With too many saints, the mind, though their heart is new, is still quite old. Their heart is full of love whereas their head is totally lacking in perception. How often the intents of the heart are utterly pure and yet the thoughts in the head are confused. Having become saturated with a mishmash of everything, the mind lacks the most signal (essential) element of all, which is spiritual insight. Countless saints genuinely love all children of God, but unfortunately their brain is stuffed with a hodgepodge of theories, opinions and objectives. Quite a number of God's best and most faithful children are the most narrow-minded and prejudice-filled. Already have they decided what is the truth and what truth they shall accept. They reject every other truth because these do not blend in with their preconceived notions. Their head is not as expansive as their heart. Moreover, there are other children of God whose mind can conceive no thought whatever. No matter how many truths have been heard they can neither remember nor practice nor communicate them to others. These have certainly heard a lot, yet they possess no ability to express any of it. For many years they have received truths, but not even a little can they supply for the needs of others. Perhaps they may even brag how full they are of the Holy Spirit! What creates such symptoms is an unrenewed mind.

THE CAUSES OF THE ATTACK OF THE EVIL SPIRITS

Why is the Christian's mental life so beset by evil spirits? this can be answered in one sentence: believers afford the evil spirits (or the devil) the opportunity to attack. Let everyone clearly understand that it is possible for one's mind to be assaulted by the devil. This is confirmed by the experience of many saints. And the area primarily assailed by him is the thinking faculty, for it has a special affinity towards evil spirits. It either partially or totally has slipped out from under man's sovereignty and has come under their dictate. Accordingly, these powers can switch one's thoughts on or off according to *their* wishes, completely disregarding the victim's ideas. Although the head is still attached to the believer, his sovereignty over it has been supplanted by another. Regardless how extensively he may protest, little can be corrected. Wherever anyone offers opportunity to wicked spirits, he cannot follow his own will any more but must be obedient to another's. When he gives ground to them in his mind he immediately forfeits his sovereignty over it. This also bespeaks the fact that his mental faculty is now being occupied by evil spirits. Had it not been attacked by them his will would continue to control everything: he could think or stop thinking as he willed without difficulty.

The most crucial factor in relation to their wicked activity is to have *ground* given to them. Without proper footing they cannot operate. The amount of their activity depends on the amount of space yielded to them. It is in the organ of his thought that the Christian supplies territory to evil spirits and hence there that they operate. Generally speaking, the ground in the mind which may be ceded to the enemy is of six kinds. We shall look at each of these now at some length.

(1) An unrenewed mind. The flesh continually furnishes bases for the enemy's operations. If man's mind is not renewed after his spirit is once regenerated, he exposes a great deal of territory to the machinations of the evil spirit. While many saints do have their mentality changed at the time of repentance, nonetheless the eyes of their heart once blinded by Satan have not yet been enlightened entirely and may still be veiled in many areas. These darkened corners are the old operation centers of the evil spirits: though greatly hindered, they have not been eliminated and thus continue to furnish bases for the operations of the unseen hosts of wickedness.

(2) An improper mind. All sins furnish territory to the adversary. If a child of God cherishes sin in his heart he is lending his mind to satanic spirits for their use. Since all sins derive from the dark powers, he is helpless to resist these powers behind whatever sins he allows to persist in his mind. As long as sinful thoughts remain in the heart, precisely that long do the evil spirits work. All unclean, proud, unkind and unrighteous ideas supply bases of activity to these spirits. Once God's child permits such a notion to stay he finds it harder to resist the next time it emerges, because the powers of darkness already have secured an area in his mind.

(3) Misunderstanding God's truth. The Lord's people rarely are aware that every time they accept a lie from the evil spirits they are furnishing fresh ground to the enemy. Should God's followers misconstrue or misinterpret as being natural or caused by their own selves that which the evil spirits have perpetrated upon their bodies, environments or works, they are yielding up precious territory to them for extending their nefarious (demonic) deeds. A lie embraced forms the ground for further activity by the satanic elements. In misunderstanding these phenomena to be the results of their own selves, they unconsciously allow these things to remain in their lives. Although this permission is gained through deceit it nevertheless provides sufficient footing for the evil spirits to operate.

(4) Accepting suggestions. Multiplied are the suggestions which Satan's hosts plant in the mind of the Christian, especially ideas concerning his circumstances and future. They enjoy prophesying to him, foretelling what will become of him and what will happen to him. Should he be unconscious of the source of such predictions and permit these to dwell in his mind, the evil spirits, at the appropriate time, will work on his environment to precipitate affairs to happen

as prophesied. Perhaps the believer may already expect it to be so, not cognizant that everything has been arranged by the enemy powers. The latter merely put their idea into the form of prophecy, then plant it in his head to see if he will accept it or reject it. Should the will of the believer raise no objection, nay, even approve of the prophecy, the spirits of wickedness have obtained a footing for enacting what they have proposed. The fulfillment of the words of fortune tellers is based entirely on this principle.

(5) A blank mind. God creates man with a mind to be used—"he who hears the word and understands it" (Matthew 13.23). God desires man to understand His Word with the intellect, from whence the emotion, will and spirit are reached. A lively head is therefore an obstacle to the work of malevolent (mischievous) spirits. One of their greatest aims is to lead a person's mind into a blank state. Blankness means an emptiness inside, the establishment of a true vacuum. The enemy powers employ either deception or force to transform the Christian's mental faculty into a blank entity. They realize that while his head is empty he cannot think. He has been stripped of all reasoning and sense and will accept without question every one of their teachings, regardless of its nature or consequence.

(6) A passive mind. Broadly speaking, an empty mind differs not too much from a passive one. Strictly speaking, the empty head means not using it whereas a passive one means awaiting some external force to activate it. The latter is a step beyond the former. Passivity is to refrain from moving by oneself and instead to let outside elements move one. A passive brain does not think by itself but allows a foreign power to do the thinking for it. Passivity reduces man to a machine.

The basic distinction between the operating requirements

of the Holy Spirit and the wicked spirits can be summarized as follows:

(1) All supernatural revelations, visions or other strange occurrences which require the *total cessation of the function of the mind*, or are obtained only after it has ceased working, are not of God.

(2) All visions which arise from the Holy Spirit are conferred when the believer's mind is fully active. It necessitates the active engagement of the various functions of the mind to apprehend these visions. The endeavors of evil spirits follow exactly the opposite course.

(3) All which flows from God agrees with God's nature and the Bible.

THE PHENOMENA OF A PASSIVE MIND

But I am afraid that, as the serpent deceived Eve by his craftiness, your mind will be led astray from the simplicity and purity of devotion to Christ.

2 Corinthians 11.3 (NASV)

It is to be sorely lamented that so many Christians, unaware of the basic difference between the activity of evil spirits and that of the Holy Spirit, have unconsciously permitted the enemy to enter and occupy their minds. Let us touch briefly on the phenomena of a mind under the attack of evil spirits.

PICTURES

The adversary also can project pictures onto the screen of a believer's mind. Some are clear and good and are welcomed by him; others are impure and sinful, much detested by his conscience. Whether good or bad, liked or disliked, the sad fact is that he has no strength to prohibit these pictures from entering his head. Against the opposition of his will, there lingers before his eyes past experiences, predictions of future events, and many other matters. This is because his power of imagination has slumped into passivity. He cannot control his imaginative powers but has allowed the evil spirits to manipulate them. The child of God should be aware that whatever does not emerge from his *own* mind proceeds from supernatural enemy forces.

DREAMS

Dreams can be natural or supernatural. Some are inspired by God while others are generated by the devil. Beyond those which are produced by man's physiological and psychological conditions, the rest are supernatural in origin. If one's mind has been open to evil spirits his night dreams become for the most part just another form of the "pictures" he encounters during the day. The wicked unseen powers create pictures in the day and dreams in the night. To determine whether or not his dreams derive from the devil the believer simply should inquire of himself: is my mind *usually* passive? If so, these dreams are untrustworthy. Moreover, dreams and visions which God inspires enable man to be normal, peaceful, steady, full of reasoning and consciousness; but what the evil spirits precipitate are bizarre, rash, fantastic, foolish, and render a person arrogant, dazed, confused, and irrational.

FORGETFULNESS

Due to the devil's attack quite a few saints are deprived of their power of memory and suffer from forgetfulness. They forget even what they have just said or done. They cannot locate the article they have just put aside that same day. They forget the promises made not so long ago. They behave as though they are without brain, for nothing seems to remain in their mind. These saints may conclude that their memory is worse than anybody else's, without realizing that their mind is actually under the disturbance of evil spirits. Consequently they must rely on notes. They become slaves to notebooks and memoranda as a means of reminder. Now we are not suggesting that a person should be able to remember everything. We grant that matters can be forgotten after many years or forgotten immediately when they leave no deep impression. Even so, many events which have happened not too long ago and which have arrested one's attention *ought* to be recalled within a certain time limit and under certain appropriate circumstances. Why are they forgotten, lost without leaving any shadow, and beyond recall? The explanation cannot be natural; it must be due to the invasion of malevolent forces. Some matters are quite naturally forgotten, others do not so naturally vanish. All unnatural loss of memory suggests the subtle attack of Satan's hosts. Many Christians undergo this kind of assault. How many endeavors are destroyed by this. And how many jokes are inspired by this forgetfulness. Confidence and usefulness are damaged.

LACK OF CONCENTRATION

Satan's minions often interfere with the Christian's power of mental concentration. We acknowledge that different individuals possess varying degrees of this power. Yet from our observations of the experiences of Christians we note that this power in most of them has suffered a greater or lesser degree of loss through the dissipating work of evil spirits. Some appear to be totally powerless to concentrate when trying to think; others are better but their thoughts take flight everywhere after but a few moments of concentration on a particular matter. Especially during times of prayer, Bible reading, or listening to messages do Christians discover their thoughts wandering. Although they will to concentrate, they fail to do so. They may succeed for a short while in arresting their galloping thoughts by their will, but such an effect does not last long. Sometimes they lose all control. It is obviously the enemy who is at work. The reason for the devil's exertions lies in the fact that the believer has made provision in his mind for the evil spirits. What a pity to see a person wasting the power of his mind, accomplishing nothing from dawn to dusk. As the wasting of physical strength is harmful, so the wasting of mental power is damaging too. Today a large number of Christians expend a great deal of time without producing much result. Their minds are assailed by evil spirits and so they cannot concentrate.

INACTIVITY

Upon being fiercely attacked, the mind of the believer loses its ability to think. It falls almost entirely into the hands of evil spirits so that he himself can no longer use it. He cannot think even should he want to, for he is incapable of initiating any thought of his own. Actually myriads of thoughts over which he has no control pass through his mind; he has no power to halt these and initiate his own. The foreign ideas are too overpowering for him to entertain his own. Occasionally he may locate an opening in his mind through which to insert his thought, but he discovers it is very toilsome to continue thinking. So many voices and so many subjects are there already that these simply squeeze his out. If any person desires to think, he must possess memory, imagination and reasoning power; but the Christian has presently lost these powers, hence is unable to think. He cannot create, deduce or recollect, nor can he compare, judge and apprehend. Therefore he cannot think. And should he attempt to do so he experiences a kind of dazed sensation which stifles any productive thought.

VACILLATION

While the mind of a believer is dominated by enemy powers his thoughts are totally unreliable, since most of them come from the wicked spirits. Few of them are his own. These spirits may generate in him one kind of thought but very shortly afterwards beget an opposite kind. In following such shifting notions the Christian naturally turns into a vacillating person. Those who are with him or work with him consider him unstable in character because he is everlastingly changing positions. Fundamentally though, it is the wicked spirits who change his thoughts and alter his opinions. How frequently we find Christians who say at one moment "I can" but at the next "I can't." They declare in the morning "I want" and shift in the afternoon to "I don't want." The reason is that at first the evil spirits plant in the mind the thought of "I can" and induce him to believe he genuinely can; nonetheless, they next inject into him another and contrary thought of "I can't" and cause him to think he really is unable. So it is not he himself who has altered what he initially declared.

OBSTINACY

After a person's mental faculty has declined into passivity and is occupied by the powers of darkness, he categorically refuses to listen to any reason or evidence once he has made a decision. He views any attempt by anyone to make him understand better as an encroachment on his liberty. He deems them most foolish, for they can never know what *he* knows! His concepts may be totally wrong, yet he thinks he has *inexplicable* reasons. Since his mind is entirely immobile, he knows not how to examine, distinguish and judge with reason. He uncritically swallows anything which the evil spirits propagate in his mind, esteeming it to be most excellent. When such an individual hears a supernatural voice he automatically accepts it as God's will; to him the voice already has become his law; it therefore transcends the investigation of reason. Whatever be the thought or voice or teaching he deems it infallible and positively safe. He refuses to test, examine, or consider; he tenaciously holds on to it and is unwilling to heed anything else. No amount of reasoning and conscience of his own or the explanation and evidence of others can move him one bit. Once he believes it to be God's leading, his mind is sealed against any change. And since he does not employ his reasoning power he can be deceived readily by evil spirits. Those who have a little understanding see the danger but he devours it all as candy. To restore such a person as this is certainly not easy.

LESSON THIRTY-THREE

THE WAY OF DELIVERANCE

. . . Laid aside the old self with its evil practices and have put on the new self who is being renewed to a true knowledge according to the image of the One who created him.

Colossians 3.9-10 (NASV)

Once knowing the truth and acknowledging that his mind has never been released or only partially released from the power of darkness, the child of God naturally will rise up to do battle against the evil spirits in order that their stronghold in him may be overthrown. Then and there he learns that the weapons of war must be spiritual, for fleshly ones avail him nothing. He cannot free himself by making resolutions or by adopting measures to improve his memory or thinking. His mind is captive to supernatural powers that cannot be cast out or destroyed by carnal devices. The believer never dreams that the powers of darkness could have so profoundly usurped his head until he learns the truth for himself and prepares to retrieve the lost territory which these wicked powers will accordingly be stirred to defend. The child of God thus comes to see how dark, dull, passive, and out of control his head truly is. The devil will use every means to torture his mind, threatening him not to take any action to recover the lost territory. This convinces the believer more than ever that his mental life is definitely a stronghold of the enemy and that he has not had complete control over it. He perceives how the enemy attempts to prevent it from understanding truths he desires to learn, for he is able to remember non-essential matters but is totally powerless to comprehend or recall the vital ones. He senses that there is an opposing force in his head which is against the truth to which he already has given consent.

Now begins the war for liberation of the mind. Is the

Christian content to remain the stronghold of the evil spirits? If not, then who must solve the problem? God? No, it is man himself. He must choose whether to offer himself wholly to God or allow his thinking apparatus to remain a concession of Satan's. Will the powers of darkness be permitted to utilize his mind? Are they going to be permitted to pour forth their perverted thoughts through the mind of the saved? Will they be allowed to fill his head with the fire from hell? Can they propagate at will their teachings through his mind? Is it henceforth going to be possible for them to resist God's truth by manipulating him in his intellect? Can they harm and torment him via the mind? The Christian himself must decide the issue. Is he willing to be a permanent puppet of the evil spirits? *He* must make the choice, else there can be no possibility of deliverance. To be sure, any decision for God does not then signify he has already overcome. It only indicates whether he is really opposing the attack of the enemy.

THE MIND RENEWED

God desires not only a change in the mind of His children at the time of conversion; He desires also a mind that is totally renewed, which is transparent as crystal. We find this commanded in the Word of God. The reason Satan can work is that the Christian has not been liberated entirely from a carnal mind. He may start out with a narrow mentality which cannot tolerate others or a darkened mentality that cannot comprehend deeper truth or a foolish mentality which cannot bear any important responsibility; and afterwards he slips into deeper sins. This is because "the mind that is set on the flesh is hostile to God" (Romans 8.7). Once knowing the teaching of Romans 6 many Christians see themselves as having already been freed from their carnal mind. What they do not appreciate is that the cross must operate minutely in every area of the man. "Consider yourselves dead to sin" must be followed by "let not

179

sin therefore reign in your mortal bodies" (Romans 6.11-12). Following the change of mentality there must be the bringing of "*every* thought captive to obey Christ" (2 Corinthians 10.5). The mind must be renewed completely, since any residue of its carnality is hostile to God.

For us to have our intellects renewed we must draw near to the cross. This is plainly called for in Ephesians 4. The Apostle Paul describes the darkness of man's carnal mentality in verses 17 and 18; but in verses 22 and 23 he informs us how the mind can be renewed: "Put off your old nature which belongs to your former manner of life and is corrupt through deceitful lusts, and be renewed in the spirit of your mind." We know our old man has been crucified with the Lord already (Romans 6.6). Here we are exhorted to "put off" so that our mind might be renewed. This brings the cross into view as the instrument for its renewal. A believer should understand that his old brain too is part of that old man which God wants us to put off entirely. The salvation which God imparts through the cross includes not only a new life but the renewal of every *function* of our soul as well. The salvation which is rooted deeply in our being must gradually be "worked out." A serious lack among Christians today is in not perceiving the need for their minds to be saved (Ephesians 6.17); they conceive salvation in general and somewhat vague terms. They fail to recognize that God desires to save them to the uttermost in that all their abilities are to be renewed and fit for His use. The mind is one of man's natural endowments. God calls His own to believe that their old man was crucified on the cross; thereafter they need to accept single-mindedly God's judgment towards the old man and exercise their will to resist or to put off its deeds including their old thoughts. They must come to the foot of the cross, willing to forsake their traditional mentalities and trusting God to give them a new mind. Brethren, the old one needs to be thoroughly put off. Yes, its renewal is God's work, but the putting off—the denial, the forsaking—of your old organ of thought is what you must do. If you perform your part, God will fulfill His. And once you put off specifically, you should just as thoroughly believe that God will renew your mind, despite the fact you know not how.

FREEDOM AND RENEWAL

As the believer retrieves the ground inch by inch, the effect gradually will be manifested. Although at the beginning situations may appear to turn worse as he attempts to recover, nonetheless if he persists he shall witness the adversary steadily losing his power. Various symptoms will decrease as the territory is increasingly regained. He will detect his mind, with its memory, imagination and reasoning powers, gradually becoming free so that he can use it again. But let him beware of one hazard at this point: he could become self-content and cease to fight to the end, to that point where all lost ground is recovered. And thus he would leave the evil spirits with a foothold for perpetrating some new future action. The believer must continue to restore his sovereignty until he is utterly emancipated. Should he stand on the foundation of the cross and exercise his mind to resist the enemy's usurpation, he shall soon be delivered completely. He shall become master of his own mental life.

Let us briefly recapitulate the process from passivity to freedom:

(1) The Christian's mind was originally normal.

(2) He sank into passivity because he wanted God to use his mind.

(3) He was deceived into thinking he now possesses a new mind.

(4) In point of fact he had fallen below normalcy through the assaults of the evil spirits.

(5) His mind grew weak and powerless.

(6) He battles to regain the lost ground.

(7) His mind seems to become more corrupt and confused than ever.

(8) Actually he is gradually regaining freedom.

(9) He insists on his sovereignty and determines to recover from his passivity.

(10) Passivity is overturned; he is recovered.

(11) By maintaining his will, he has not only succeeded in thereafter retaining his normalcy, but also

(12) His mind is so recovered that he can do what he could not do before.

Let us see that a renewed mind is something deeper than simply a freed one. To regain the strongholds forfeited through passivity and believing the enemy's lie means merely to restore what has been lost; but to be renewed includes not only restoration of what was relinquished but also a coming into possession of something higher than he originally had. To have a mind renewed is to arrive at the highest possibility which God has ordained for his mind. God wants the Christian's mind not just to be unshackled from the power of darkness by becoming wholly self-controlled, but in addition to be *renewed* so that it can cooperate completely with the Holy Spirit. God desires the mind to be full of light, wisdom and understanding, with all its imaginations and reasonings purified and brought to perfect obedience to God's will (Colossians 1.9). Let us therefore not be content with but a little gain.

THE LAWS OF THE MIND

For the mind set on the flesh is death, but the mind set on the Spirit is life and peace.

Romans 8.6 (NASV)

In analyzing the discerning-understanding-performing process of a *spiritual* Christian, we can identify these steps: (1) the Holy Spirit reveals God's will in one's spirit that he may know what it is; (2) through his mind he comprehends the meaning of this revelation; and (3) with his volition he engages his spiritual strength to activate the body that it may execute God's will. Nothing in a person's life is closer to the spirit than his mind. We know it is the mechanism for learning matters in the intellectual and material realms while the spirit is the component for perceiving realities in the spiritual realm. A Christian knows all things about himself through the intellect whereas he knows the things of God through the spirit. Both are organs of knowledge, hence their relationship is manifestly closer than are others. In walking after the spirit we shall find the mind to be the best helper to the spirit. It is therefore necessary to understand how these two work together.

The Bible speaks most distinctly about the coordination of the spirit and the mind: "that the God of our Lord Jesus Christ, the Father of glory, may give you a spirit of wisdom and of revelation in the *knowledge* of him, having the eyes of your hearts enlightened, that you may *know* . . ." (Ephesians 1.17-18). We have explained the meaning of "a spirit of wisdom and of revelation" before; it means that God makes Himself and His will known to us by giving revelation in our spirit. But now we wish to note how the revelation obtained intuitively in our spirit works together with our mind.

"The eyes of your heart" points figuratively to the organ of our reasoning and understanding, that is, our mind. In this passage the word "know" or "knowledge"—used twice—serves to convey two distinctive notions: the first one is a knowing intuitively, the second is a knowing or understanding mentally. This spirit of revelation is located in the depth of our being. God reveals Himself to our spirit that we may truly apprehend Him by our intuition. Thus far, however, this is but intuitive knowledge; that is to say, the inner man knows while the outer man remains ignorant. The communication to the outward man of what has been known by the inward man is an indispensable step, the lack of which prevents united action by the inner and outer man together. How then can there be this communication? The Scripture informs us that our spirit will enlighten our mental faculty to make it understand the meaning of the revelation in the intuition. Since our outward man depends on the mind in order to comprehend things, the spirit must convey what it knows intuitively to the mind so that the latter can deliver the message to the entire being and enable the child of God to walk according to the spirit.

We first come to know the will of God in our intuition and then our intellect interprets that will to us. The Holy Spirit moves in our spirit, producing in us a spiritual sense; afterwards we exercise our brain to study and to understand the meaning of this sense. It requires the cooperation of both spirit and mind to comprehend fully the will of God. The spirit enables our inner man to know, while the mind causes our outer man to understand. Such cooperation occurs in a second, although it takes longer to describe with pen and ink. They operate like two hands: and in the twinkling of an eye the spirit already has made known to the mind what it has seen. All revelations come from the Holy Spirit and are received not by the mind but by man's spirit, so that man may know by intuition; they are then studied and understood by his mental powers.

We consistently ought to refuse to allow the mind to serve

as the prime element for receiving God's will, yet we must not inhibit it from serving as the secondary apparatus for understanding that will. A carnal Christian mistakes the thought of the head to be the criterion for his conduct because he has not yet learned how to walk after the spirit. A spiritual Christian follows the spirit, but he also permits his mind to comprehend what the spirit means. In true guidance these two elements are one. Ordinarily the leading in the spirit opposes what men call reasoning; however, to the person whose rational power has been renewed such reasoning works together with his spirit, thus his guidance seems perfectly logical to *his* reasoning. But the rationality of the person whose inner man has not yet attained this lofty position frequently will withstand the leading of the spirit.

MIND, THE SPIRIT, AND A SPIRITUAL MIND

The more spiritual a child of God becomes the more he is conscious of the significance of walking according to the spirit and the dangers of walking according to the flesh. But how is he actually to walk by the spirit? The answer given in Romans 8 is to mind the spirit and to possess a spiritual mind: "they that are after the flesh mind the things of the flesh; but they that are after the Spirit the things of the Spirit. For the mind of the flesh is death; but the mind of the Spirit is life and peace" (vv. 5-6 ASV). To walk after the spirit means to have the mind set on the things of the Spirit; it also means to have the spirit rule the mind. Those who act according to the spirit are none other than those who are occupied with the things of the inner man and whose mind is therefore spiritual. Walking by the spirit simply denotes that a mind under the control of the spirit sets itself on the things of the spirit. This implies that our mentality has been renewed and has become spirit-controlled and thus qualified to detect every movement and silence of the spirit.

Why is *minding* the realities of the spirit so important to a life which walks after the spirit? Because that is the most conspicuous condition for securing guidance in the spirit. How many of God's children wait for Him to arrange their circumstances while concomitantly overlooking the need to heed the spirit; that is, they pay no heed to the prompting of their inner depths. Often God Who indwells us already has led us within our spirit, yet because of the dullness of our mental faculty we just do not appreciate it. He has truly given revelation to our intuition, but our intellect is dwelling on a thousand and one matters other than on the movement in the spirit. We are neglecting our spiritual sense. Sometimes our spirit is normal but our mind errs, so we are incapacitated from following the spirit. Whatever is expressed by its intuition is delicate, quiet and gentle; unless we habitually mind its realities, how can we ever know the thought of the spirit and accordingly walk? Our mind ought to be alert like a watchman, always on the lookout for the movement in the inner man so that our outer man may be yielded wholly.

AN OPEN MIND

Besides experiencing God's direct revelation, we also frequently receive truth through the preaching of the Word by other children of God. Such truth is first received in the intellect before it reaches the spirit. Since we make contact with the utterances or writings of others with the mind, there is hardly any possibility of this kind of truth reaching our life except through the channel of the mind. An open mind is consequently of paramount importance to spiritual life. If our brain is full of prejudice towards the truth or towards the preacher, truth will not enter it nor will it extend to our life. No wonder some believers derive no help—already have they decided what they would like to read or hear.

A CONTROLLED MIND

Every part of the Christian's life needs to be under reins;

that includes the mind even following its renewal. We ought not toss the reins to it lest the evil spirits take advantage. Let us remember that *thought is the seed of action*. Carelessness here invariably leads to sin there. An idea sown will eventually grow, however prolonged such growth may require. We can trace all our presumptuous and unconscious sins to those seed thoughts we allowed to be planted before. If a sinful notion is allowed to stay in the head, then after a time, perhaps a few years, it will result in a sinful act. Suppose, for example, we conceive an evil thought against a certain brother. If it is not eradicated and cleansed immediately, it ultimately will produce its unsavory fruit. The Christian must exert his utmost strength to deal with his thoughts. Should his mental life be left uncontrolled, he cannot possibly control anything. Hence Peter exhorts us to "gird up (our) minds" (1 Peter 1.13), by which he means to say that we must regulate all our thoughts and never let them run wild.

God's objective is to "take *every* thought captive to obey Christ." Hence we ought to scrutinize every one of our thoughts in the light of God, not allowing one to escape our observation or judgment. Whatever the notion may be, it must be examined and controlled.

A MIND FULL OF GOD'S WORD

"I will put my laws into their minds," declares God (Hebrews 8.10). We should read and memorize more of the Word of God, lest we be unable to find it at the moment of urgent need. If we diligently read the Bible, God will fill every thought of ours with His laws. We shall recall instantly what the Bible says when we are in need of light for our way. Many are unwilling to exercise their minds in reading the Word. They like to open the Bible at random following prayer and take whatever is before them as being from God. This is extremely untrustworthy. But if our mind is abounding in His Word, the Holy Spirit is able through our spirit's intuition to enlighten our mind at once by bringing to our remembrance some appropriate verse. We do not require anyone to tell us we should not steal, for we know the Word of God has said so. Such a word is already in our mind. This is true in other matters as well; so if we are united with the Bible in this way, we shall be able to apprehend the mind of God in all regards.

LESSON THIRTY-FIVE

A BELIEVER'S WILL

Not my will, but Yours be done.

Luke 22.42 (NASV)

A man's will is his organ for decision-making. To want or not to want, to choose or not to choose are the typical operations of the will. It is his "helm" by which he sails upon the sea of life.

The will of a man can be taken as his real self, for it truthfully represents him. Its action is the action of the man. When we declare "*I* will," it is actually our volition which wills. When we say "*I* want, *I* decide," again it is our volition which wants and decides. Our volition acts for the entire man. Our emotion merely expresses how we feel; our mind simply tells us what we think; but our will communicates what we *want*. Hence, it is the most influential component of our entire person. It is deeper than emotion and mind. So in seeking spiritual growth the believer must not neglect the volitional element in him.

True and perfect salvation saves man's will. Whatever is not sufficiently thorough to embrace the salvation of man's volition is but vanity. All pleasant feelings and all lucid thoughts belong exclusively to the external realm. Man may experience joy, comfort and peace in believing God, he may understand His majesty and amass much wonderful knowledge; but does he possess any genuine union with Him if his will is not united with God's? The joining of wills forms the only true union. Consequently, upon receiving life the believer should be attentive not only to his intuition but likewise to his volition.

THE FALL AND SALVATION

Unfortunately, mankind has fallen. By this plunge man's unfettered volition suffered prodigious (extensive) damage.

189

We may say that there are two massive contradictory wills throughout the universe. On the one side stands the holy and perfect will of God; on the other is arrayed the defiled, defiling and opposing will of Satan. In between subsists the sovereign, independent, free will of man. When man listens to the devil and rebels against God he seems to render an eternal "no" to God's will and an abiding "yes" to Satan's. Since man employs his volition to choose the will of the devil, his volition falls captive to the devil. Therefore all his acts are governed by Satan's will. Until he overturns his early subjection, man's will remains unquestionably oppressed by the enemy power.

In this fallen position and condition man is fleshly. This flesh—by which his will, together with his other organs, is ruled—is thoroughly corrupted. How can anything pleasing to God ever result from such a darkened will? Even his questing after God springs from the realm of the flesh and therefore lacks any spiritual value. He may invent many ways of worshiping God at this time, yet all are his own ideas, all are "will-worship" (Colossians 2.23 ASV), totally unacceptable to Him.

A SUBMISSIVE WILL

What is salvation? It is none other than God saving man out of himself into Himself. Salvation has two facets: a cutting off and a uniting with. What is cut off is self; the uniting is with God. Whatever does not aim at deliverance from self and union with Him is not genuine salvation. Anything which cannot save man from self and join him to God is vanity. A true spiritual beginning involves release from animal life (natural life) and entry into divine life. Everything belonging to the created one must be relinquished so that the created one will enjoy all things solely in the Creator. The created one must vanish in order that true salvation may be manifested. Real greatness rests not on how much we have but on how much we have lost. Authentic life can be seen only in the abandonment of self. If the nature, life and activities of the created one are not denied, the life of God has no way to express itself. Our "self" is often the enemy of God's life. Our spiritual growth shall be stunted severely if we have no intention nor experience of losing ourselves.

What is self? That is extremely difficult to answer, nor can our answer be fully correct. But were we to say "self" is "self-will," we would not be too far from the mark. Man's essence is in his volition because it expresses what man fundamentally is, desires, and is willing for. Before God's grace has done its work in man all which a man has, whether he be sinner or saint, is generally contrary to God. It is because man belongs to the natural, which is exceedingly antithetical (opposed) to God's life.

Salvation, then, is to deliver man from his created, natural, animal, fleshly, and self-emanating will. Let us make a special note of this: that aside from God giving us a new life, the turning of our will to Him is the greatest work in salvation. We may even say that God imparts new life in order for us to abandon our will to Him. The gospel is to facilitate the union of our will with God. Anything short of this is failure of the mission. God aims his arrow of salvation not so much at our emotion or our mind but at our will, for once the latter is saved, the rest are included.

TWO MEASURES

Two measures are necessary in being joined to God in will. The first is for God to subdue the activities of our will; the second is to conquer the life of our will. Quite often our volition is subservient to the Lord only in a number of particular matters, which nonetheless prompts us to think that we are fully obedient to Him. Down within us, however, hides a secret tendency which shall rise to the surface when the opportunity is provided. God's intent is not merely to curtail the movement of our will but also to smash its inner tendency so that its very quality seems to be transformed. Strictly speaking, an obedient will and a harmonious one are very different: obedience is related to activity whereas harmony is related to life, nature and tendency. The obedient will of a servant is seen in his executing every order of his master, but the son who knows the father's heart and whose will is one with the father's not only fulfills his duty but fulfills it *with delight* as well. An obedient will puts a stop to one's own activity, yes, but a harmonious will is in addition one heart with God. Only those who are in harmony with Him can actually appreciate his heart. If a person has not arrived at this perfect harmony between his own and God's will, he has yet to experience the summit of spiritual life. To be obedient to the Lord is indeed good, but when grace completely conquers the natural life the Christian will be fully attuned to Him. As a matter of fact, the union of wills is the zenith of anyone's spiritual walk.

PASSIVITY AND ITS DANGERS

For God has not given us a spirit of timidity but of power and love and discipline.

2 Timothy 1.7 (NASV)

What primarily precipitates the enemy's invasion among the "heathen" and among carnal Christians is willful sin; but "the primary cause of deception . . . in surrendered believers may be condensed into one word, passivity; that is, *a cessation of the active exercise of the will in control over spirit, soul, and body, or either, as may be the case.*" The organ of volition ceases to choose and decide matters referred to it. "The word passivity simply describes the opposite condition to activity; and in the experience of the believer it means, briefly, (1) loss of self-control—in the sense of the person himself controlling each, or all, of the departments of his personal being; and (2) loss of free-will—in the sense of the person himself exercising his will as the guiding principle of personal control, in harmony with the will of God." The passivity of a saint arises out of the non-use of his various talents. He has a mouth but refuses to talk because he hopes the Holy Spirit will speak through it. He has hands but will not engage them since he expects God to do it. He does not exercise any part of his person but waits for God to move him. He considers himself fully surrendered to God; so he no longer will *use* any element of his being. Thus he falls into an inertia which opens the way for deception and invasion.

Upon accepting the teaching of their union with God's will, Christians often develop a wrong concept of what this union signifies. They misconstrue it to mean to obey God passively. They think their will must be cancelled out and that they must become puppets. They maintain that they must not employ their own volition any more nor that their will should exercise control over any other segment of their body. They no longer choose, decide, or activate with their will. At first it appears to be a great victory, for amazingly "the 'strong-willed' person suddenly becomes passively yielding." (Penn-Lewis, *War on the Saints,* 73) He is as weak as water. He holds no opinion on any affair but obeys orders absolutely. He exercises neither mind, nor will, nor even conscience to distinguish between good and evil, for he is a person of perfect obedience. Only when he is moved does he move; a perfect condition (and an invitation too) for the enemy to come in.

Here then is the antithesis between the working of God and the working of Satan. Though God wants man to be yielded completely to Him, He also wants him to use every talent he possesses in cooperation with the Holy Spirit. Satan, on the other hand, demands total cessation of man's will and actions that his evil spirits may operate in his stead. The contrast is truly sobering: God calls man to choose actively, consciously and willingly to do His will so that his spirit, soul, and body may be free; Satan coerces him to be his passive slave and captive: God appoints man to be autonomous, free to be his own master; Satan forces man to be his puppet, a marionette altogether manipulated by him: God never requires man to cease his activities before He can work; Satan bids man to be utterly passive and inactive: God asks man to work together with Him consciously; Satan charges man to obey him passively. It is true that God does require man to cease from his every sinful activity without which he cannot cooperate with the Holy Spirit; but Satan compels him to cease *all* his activities, including the functioning of his soul, so that his minions can act in place of man. Man is thus reduced to a mere piece of machinery without any conscious responsibility.

THE DANGERS

A Christian in his ignorance may be deceived by the powers of darkness, may unwittingly tumble into the trap of Satan, and fulfill the conditions for his working. Let us observe the order of this process, for it is highly important: (1) ignorance, (2) deception, (3) passivity, and (4) entrenchment. Ignorance is the primary cause of this process. Satan can deceive because the saint is unfamiliar both with the demand of the Holy Spirit and the principle of satanic working. Were Christians to apprise themselves of how to cooperate with God and what His procedure of working is, they would never accept Satan's deception. But once deceived, they surmise that for God to live and work through them means for them to remain passive; and so they accept as being from God many supernatural manifestations from evil spirits. The deception grows deeper, finally resulting in an entrenchment of alarming proportions.

It is a vicious cycle: each time ground is given, the evil spirits are encouraged to come in; upon entering, they manifest themselves through sundry activities; and if the believer misinterprets these activities, not knowing that they originate with the devil, he will cede even more place to the evil spirits since he has believed already in their lies. This cycle goes round and round, daily augmenting the degree of penetration. Once he descends into passivity by furnishing a foothold to evil spirits, the dangers can easily multiply.

LESSON THIRTY-SEVEN

THE BELIEVER'S MISTAKE

My people are destroyed for lack of knowledge.

Hosea 3.6a (NASV)

We must not fall under the misapprehension that those believers who are deceived by evil spirits must be the most defiled, degenerate, and sinful. They are on the contrary oftentimes fully surrendered Christians spiritually more advanced than ordinary believers. They strive to obey God and are willing to pay any cost. Unwittingly do they stumble into passivity because of the fact that although they are wholly consecrated they know not how to cooperate with God. Those who are less serious about spiritual matters do not face the danger of passivity, for how could anyone sink into inactivity and eventually into the grip of the enemy when, though professing to be utterly consecrated, he persists in living according to his own ideas? He might give ground to evil spirits in other respects but certainly not in the matter of yielding to God's will by delivering a passive ground to the enemy. Only those committed ones who disregard their own interests are open to passivity. Their will can easily slip into this state since they are most eager to obey all orders.

Many will wonder why God does not protect them. Is not their motive pure? How can God permit such faithful seekers of His to be deceived by evil spirits? Many people will contend that He ought to safeguard His Own children under any circumstance; they do not realize that to enjoy God's protection one must fulfill His conditions for protection. Should a person fulfill the conditions for the working of the evil spirits God cannot forbid the latter to work, for He is a law-abiding One. Because the Christian intentionally or unintentionally has surrendered himself to the evil spirits God will not hinder them from the right to control that one. How many hold to the idea that a pure motive safeguards them from deception! Little do they realize that the people most deceived in the world are those with good intentions. Honesty is no condition for not being deceived; but *knowledge* is. Should the believer neglect the teaching of the Bible, failing to watch and pray even though trusting his pure motive to keep him from deception, he shall be deceived. How can he expect God to protect him when he is providing the pre-requisites for the working of evil spirits?

Countless saints consider themselves beyond deception because they have had frequent spiritual experiences. This very element of self-confidence betrays the deception they are in already. Unless they are humble enough to acknowledge the possibility of being deceived, they shall be deceived perpetually. Deception is neither a matter of life nor of intention but one of knowledge. It is difficult for the Holy Spirit to point out the truth to that person who has absorbed too many idealistic teachings in the early stages of his Christian experience. Equally hard is it for others to supply him with necessary light if he already has developed a prejudiced interpretation of the Scriptures. The danger of such false security is to give opportunity for the evil spirits to work or to continue to work.

A MISTAKEN NOTION CONCERNING CO-DEATH WITH CHRIST

The conditions for passivity in a believer may come about through a wrong interpretation concerning the truth of "death with Christ." Paul says that "I have been crucified with Christ; it is no longer I who live, but Christ who lives in me; and the life I now live in the flesh I live by faith in the Son of God, who loved me and gave himself for me" (Galatians 2.20). Some misconstrue this to connote self-effacement. What they deem to be the summit of spiritual life is "a loss of personality, an absence of volition and self control, and the passive letting-go of the 'I myself' into a condition of machine-like, mechanical, automatic 'obedience'" (Penn-Lewis, *War on the Saints*, 86). They thereafter must harbor no feelings; they should instead renounce all consciousness of personal wishes, interests and tastes. They must aim at self-annihilation, reducing themselves to corpses. Their personality must be totally eclipsed. They misapprehend the command of God to mean a demand for their self-effacement, self-renunciation and self-annihilation so they may no longer be aware of themselves or their needs but may be conscious only of the movement and operation of God in them. Their misconception about being "dead to self" means for them the absence of self-consciousness. So they endlessly deliver their self-consciousness to nought till they sense nothing but the presence of God. Under this mistaken notion they assume they must practice death; on each occasion therefore when they become aware of "self" or are conscious of personal wants, lacks, needs, interests or preferences they consistently consign these to death.

GOD'S WORKING

Another text easily mishandled is Philippians 2.13: "it is God who worketh in you both to will and to work, for his good pleasure" (ASV). To some this passage seems to teach that God performs both the willing and the working; that is, that He puts into His child what He has willed and worked. Since God wills and works instead of him, he himself need not do so. The believer has become a kind of superior creature having no need to will and to do work now that God has done so for him. He is like a mechanical toy which exercises no responsibility of its own to will and do. These saints do not see that the correct substance of this verse is that God works in us up to the point of our readiness to will and to work. He undertakes only to that point and no farther. He never wills or acts in place of man. He merely endeavors to bring man to the position of being disposed to will and to do His excellent will.

THE WORK OF THE HOLY SPIRIT

Believers think Acts 5.32 suggests that they must obey the Holy Spirit—"the Holy Spirit whom God has given to those who obey him." But they fail, according to the command given in the Bible, to test all the spirits to see if they are of truth or of error (1 John 4.1, 6). They instead accept as being the Holy Spirit every spirit which comes to them. They think this obedience must be highly pleasing to God. What they do not know is that the Scripture here does not teach us to obey the Holy Spirit but to obey God the Father through the Spirit. In verse 29 of Acts 5 the Apostles when under questioning by the council replied that they "must obey *God*." Should anyone make God the Spirit his object of obedience and forget God the Father he tends to obey the spirit in him or around him instead of obeying through the Holy Spirit the Father Who is in heaven. This will set him on the road to passivity and in addition provide the evil spirits the chance for counterfeit. Overstepping the bounds of the Word of God ushers in countless perils!

SPIRITUAL LIFE

"And your ears shall hear a word behind you, saying, 'This is the way, walk in it'" (Isaiah 30.21). Saints do not perceive that this verse refers specifically to the experience of God's earthly people, the Jews, during the millennial kingdom when there shall be no satanic counterfeit. Unaware of this fact they view supernatural guidance in a voice to be the highest form of guidance. They esteem themselves more spiritual than the rest and hence receive supernatural guidance of this type. They neither listen to their conscience nor follow their intuition; they merely wait in a passive manner for the supernatural voice. These believers hold that they do not need to think, ponder, choose or decide. They simply need to obey. They permit the voice to be substituted for their intuition and conscience. And the consequence is that "(a) he does not use his conscience; (b) God does not speak to him for automatic obedience; (c) evil spirits take the opportunity and supernatural voices are substituted for the action of the conscience" (Penn-Lewis, WOTS, 121). The outcome is that the enemy gains more ground in the believer. And "from this time (forward) the man is not influenced by what he feels or sees, or by what others say, and he closes himself to all questions, and will not reason. This substitution of supernatural guidance for the action of the conscience explains the deterioration of the moral standard in persons with supernatural experiences, because they have really substituted the direction of evil spirits for their conscience. They are quite unconscious that their moral standard is lowered, but their conscience has become seared by deliberately ceasing to heed its voice; and by listening to the voices of the teaching spirits, in matters which should be decided by the conscience in respect to their being right or wrong, good or evil" (Penn-Lewis, WOTS, 121-22).

GOD'S ORDERING

We know that besides man's will there are two other totally antagonistic wills in the world. God calls us to obey Him and to resist Satan. Twice in the Bible do we find these two sides mentioned together: (1) "submit yourselves therefore to God," exhorts James, and then he follows immediately with "resist the devil" (4.7); (2) "humble yourselves therefore under the mighty hand of God," enjoins Peter, and continues by charging his readers to "resist (the devil), firm in your faith" (1 Peter 5.6, 9). This is the balance of truth. A believer certainly must learn to submit himself to God in all matters, acknowledging that what He orders for him is the best. Though he suffers, yet he heartily submits to the will of God. This, however, is just *half* the truth. The Apostles understood the danger of being lopsided; hence we find them right away warning the Christian to resist the devil once he submits to God. This is because there is another will besides His, that of Satan's. Frequently the devil counterfeits the will of God, especially in the things which happen to us. If we are unaware of the presence of a will other than God's, we can easily mistake Satan's to be God's and so fall into the devil's trap. For this reason God wants us to resist the devil when we submit to Him. Resistance is done by the *will*. Resistance means our volition opposes, disapproves, and withstands. God wishes us to exercise our volition, therefore He exhorts us to "resist the devil." He will not resist for us; we ourselves must do so. We have a will; we should use it to take heed to God's Word. So teaches the Bible. Thinking that God's will is revealed in His orderings, the Christian may accept anything which comes to him as His will. In that event he naturally will not employ his volition to choose, decide or resist. He just quietly accepts everything. This sounds good and appears right, but it contains a serious fallacy.

LESSON THIRTY-EIGHT

THE PATH TO FREEDOM

And you will know the truth, and the truth will make you free.

John 8.32 (NASV)

The very first step to freedom is to know the truth of all things: truth concerning cooperation with God, the operation of evil spirits, consecration, and supernatural manifestations. The child of God must know the truth as to the source and nature of the experiences he may have been having if he expects to be delivered. Since his descent was (1) deception, (2) passivity, (3) entrenchment, and (4) further deception and passivity, then the way to release will be initially the uncovering of deception. Once the early deceit is dissolved, passivity, entrenchment and further deceit will disintegrate. Deception unlatches the gate for the evil spirits to rush in; passivity provides a place for them to stay; and the result of these two is entrenchment. To dispossess them requires an ending of passivity which in turn needs the exposure of deception, and this is brought about by nothing else save the knowledge of truth. Knowledge of truth is therefore the first stage towards freedom. Only the truth can set people free.

We have cautioned our readers repeatedly about the danger of supernatural experience. We are not suggesting that every such manifestation must be categorically resisted, forsaken and opposed: this would be at variance with Biblical teaching since the Scriptures record numerous supernatural acts of God. Our purpose simply has been to remind Christians that there can be more than one source behind supernatural phenomena; God can perform wonders, but so can evil spirits imitate! How crucial for us to distinguish what is of God from what is not of God. If one has not died to his emotional life but earnestly seeks sensational events, he will be easily duped. We do not urge people to resist all supernatural manifestations, but we do exhort them to resist every supernatural occurrence which derives from Satan. So what we have tried to point out throughout this part of the book has been the basic differences between the operation of the Holy Spirit and that of the evil spirit so as to help God's children discern which is which.

The roads to truth are many and various. Some are awakened to their true state upon discovering that they have lost their liberty in all respects through their protracted and serious satanic bondage; others whose experiences may be ninety per cent of God and only ten per cent impurity come to know the truth when they begin to doubt their experience; still others are brought to a knowledge of their condition through the truth given them by other believers. In any event, the Christian should not refuse the first ray of light which shines upon him.

Doubting is the prelude to truth. By this is not meant to doubt the Holy Spirit or God or His Word but to doubt one's own past experience. Such doubt is both necessary and scriptural because God commands us to "test the spirits" (1 John 4.1). Believers often embrace a wrong idea: they are afraid to examine the spirits lest they sin against the Holy Spirit. But it is He Himself Who desires us to make the test. Now if it turns out to be the Holy Spirit He can stand the test; if however it is the evil spirit its true nature will accordingly be exposed. Is it God Who has in fact caused you to fall into today's position? Does the Holy Spirit ever work contrary to His law? Are you really infallible in all matters?

Having received some light as to the truth, the believer next can readily admit that he is susceptible to deception. And this affords the truth a working opportunity. The worst fallacy one can ever commit is to reckon oneself infallible. To maintain that others may be wrong but never he is to be duped to the very end. Only after he is self-abased will he be able to see that he is genuinely deceived. By comparing the principle of divine working against the conditions of satanic working, he concludes that his past experiences were obtained through passivity. He had fulfilled the requirements for the working of the evil spirits, hence was given those many strange manifestations which made him happy initially but which pained him ultimately. He had not cooperated actively with God but had instead passively followed that will which he had taken for granted must be God's. Both his happy and painful experiences must have originated with evil spirits. He consequently now admits how deceived he has been. The child of God not only must accept the truth but in addition must admit his condition in the light of that truth. In this way the lie of the enemy shall be annulled. Thus one's experience here is to (a) acknowledge that a *believer* is open to deception; (b) admit that *he* too is subject to duplicity; (c) confess that *he* is deceived; and next (d) further inquire as to why he was beguiled.

Upon realizing he has been deceived, the believer should next seek light concerning the ground he has lost and try to recover it. Since evil spirits maintain their position on the territory surrendered to them, they shall leave once that area is cleared away.

One common principle underlies the way all ground is relinquished to evil spirits: it is through passivity, the inactivity of the will. If lost ground is ever to be recovered it is mandatory that the volition be reactivated. The Christian henceforth must learn (a) to obey God's will, (b) to resist the devil's will, and (c) to exercise his own will in collaboration with the will of the other saints. Responsibility for recovering ceded territory rests chiefly on the will. It is the volition which became passive, hence it must be the volition which dispels passivity.

The first measure the will undertakes is to *resolve*, that is, to set itself towards a definite direction. Having suffered much at the hands of evil spirits but now enlightened by the truth and encouraged by the Holy Spirit, the child of God is led naturally to a new position of abhorring those wicked spirits. He accordingly resolves against all their works. He is determined to regain his freedom, be his own master, and drive off his enemy. The Spirit of God so works in him that his fury against the evil spirits gathers momentum. The more he suffers the more he hates; the more he ponders his plight the more furious he becomes. He resolves to experience a complete emancipation from the powers of darkness. Such a resolve is the first step towards the recovery of lost ground. If this resolution is real he will press on towards the goal no matter how fierce a fight the enemy may put up. The entire man supports his resolve to henceforth oppose the adversary.

The child of God must reclaim all footholds until he arrives at the freedom he first enjoyed. He should know *from where* he has fallen since it is to that place that he must be restored. He ought to understand what was hitherto normal for him— how active his will and how clear his mind were in the beginning—as well as what his current condition is. By comparing these two states he will be able to ascertain how far he has descended into passivity. Whatever his normal state was, that must he now set before himself as the minimum standard or goal of his ascent. He should not be satisfied until his will is restored to its original state, that is, until it actively controls every part of his being. He should never deem himself free before his normalcy has once more been regained.

"The 'fighting through' period is a very painful time. There are bad moments of acute suffering, and intense struggle, arising out of the consciousness of the resistance of the powers of darkness in their contest for what the believer endeavors to reclaim" (Penn-Lewis, *War on the Saints*, 194). In exercising his volition to (a) resist the rule of the evil spirits and (b) reinstate his own office, the Christian shall meet stiff opposition from his enemy. Initially he may not be aware of the depth to which he has fallen; but once he commences,

point by point, to fight his way back to a normal state, then does he discover how far he has plunged. Because of the resistance of the enemy he may find at the initial stage of combat that his symptoms grow *worse* than before, as though the more he fights the less strength his will has and the more confused becomes the particular area over which the engagement is being fought. Such a phenomenon is nonetheless the sign of *victory*! Though the believer does feel worse, in reality he is better. *For it demonstrates that the resistance has had its effect: the enemy has felt the pressure and is consequently making his last stand. If one continues to exert the pressure the evil spirits will depart.*

During the battle it is positively essential that the believer stand on Romans 6.11, acknowledging himself as *one* with the Lord: the Lord's death is his death. Such faith releases him from the authority of the evil spirits since they can have no power over the dead. This position must be firmly taken. In conjunction with such a stand as this there must be the use of God's Word against all the lies of the enemy, because at this juncture the adversary will lie to the saint by suggesting that he has fallen beyond any hope of restoration. If he listens to this guile he will surely tumble into the greatest peril of all. He should remind himself that Calvary has destroyed Satan and his evil hosts already (Hebrews 2.14; Colossians 2.14-15). The work of salvation is finished that all may experience deliverance out of the powers of darkness into the kingdom of the Son of God's love (Colossians 1.13). Suffering for the sake of recovering ground assures a person of that which the enemy is afraid of, and how urgent that the ground be recovered. Consequently, whenever the wicked powers inflict new and greater afflictions upon the believer, let him perceive that these are from the enemy and then let him refuse and disregard them, neither worrying nor talking about them.

THE BELIEVER AND HIS BODY

The body is not meant for immorality, but for the Lord, and the Lord for the body.

1 Corinthians 6.13b

We should know what place our physical body occupies in the purpose and plan of God. Can anyone deny the relationship between the body and spirituality? In addition to a spirit and a soul we also have a body. However healthy may be the intuition, communion and conscience of our spirit and however renewed the emotion, mind and will of our soul, we can never develop into spiritual men and women—never be perfected but continually lacking in some way—if our body is not as sound and restored as are our spirit and soul. We should not neglect our outer shell while attending to our inner components. Our life shall suffer if we commit this blunder.

The body is necessary and important; otherwise God would not have created man with one. By accurately searching the Scriptures we can discover how much attention God pays to man's body, for the Bible has a lot to say about it. Most singular and awesome of all is the fact that the Word became flesh: the Son of God took upon Himself a body of flesh and blood: and though He died He wears this garb forever.

THE HOLY SPIRIT AND THE BODY

Romans 8.10-13 unfolds to us the condition of our body, how the Holy Spirit helps it, and what ought to be our right attitude towards it. If we appropriate these verses we will not misunderstand the place of a believer's body in God's plan of redemption.

"If Christ is in you, although your bodies are dead because of sin, your spirits are alive because of righteousness" (v.10).

207

Initially both our body and spirit were dead; but after we believed in the Lord Jesus we received Him into us to be our life. The fact that Christ by the Holy Spirit lives in the believer forms one of the essential tenets of the gospel. Every child of God, however weak, has Christ dwelling in him. This Christ is our life. And when He enters to make His abode in us, our spirit is made alive. Formerly both the spirit and the body were dead; now the spirit is quickened, leaving only the body dead. The estate common to *every believer* is that his body is dead but his spirit is alive.

"If the Spirit of him who raised Jesus from the dead dwells in you, he who raised Christ Jesus from the dead will give life to your mortal bodies also through his Spirit which dwells in you" (v.11). Verse 10 explains how God quickens our spirit; this verse tells us how God gives life to our body. The tenth verse speaks of the spirit being made alive, with the body still dead; the eleventh verse goes further by saying that after the spirit is made alive the body too may live. The first part announces that the spirit lives because of Christ dwelling in us; this part declares that the body will live because of the Holy Spirit abiding in us. The Holy Spirit will give life to our bodies.

By this verse God informs His children of their bodily privilege, which is life to their mortal frames through His Spirit Who indwells them. It does not assert that the "body of sin" has become a holy body or that our "lowly body" has been transformed into a glorious one or that this mortal body has put on immortality. These cannot be realized in this life. The redemption of our earthen vessels must wait till the Lord comes and receives us to Himself. To change the nature of our body in this age is impossible. Therefore the real meaning of the Holy Spirit giving life to our bodies is that: (1) He will restore us when we are sick and (2) He will preserve us if we are not sick. In a word, the Holy Spirit will strengthen our earthly tents so that we can meet the requirements of God's work and walk in order that neither our life nor the kingdom of God will suffer through the weakness of the body.

GLORIFY GOD

The passage in 1 Corinthians 6.12-20 sheds additional light on this matter of the believer's body. Let us consider this passage verse by verse.

"All things are lawful for me, but not all things are helpful. All things are lawful for me, but I will not be enslaved by anything" (v.12). As substantiated by the verses following, the Apostle Paul is here writing about the body. He judges all things to be lawful because according to nature every demand of the body—such as eating, drinking or sex—is natural, reasonable and lawful (v.13). Yet he further judges that not every one of them is necessarily helpful nor should any enslave man. In other words, according to man's natural existence the Christian may be permitted to do many things with his body, but as one who belongs to God he is additionally able *not* to do these things for the glory of God.

"Food is meant for the stomach and the stomach for food— and God will destroy both one and the other. The body is not meant for immorality, but for the Lord, and the Lord for the body" (v.13). The first half of this verse corresponds to the first half of the preceding verse. Food is lawful, but since food and stomach will eventually be destroyed, none is eternally useful. The latter half of the verse corresponds to that half of the preceding verse too. The Christian is capable of rising completely above the urge of sex and yielding his body wholly to the Lord (1 Corinthians 7.34).

"The body is for the Lord." This is a word having enormous import. Paul is speaking to us firstly about the issue of food. In the matter of eating and drinking the Christian is afforded a chance to prove in practice that "the body is for the Lord." Man originally fell on this very point of food; the Lord Jesus was tempted in the wilderness on this same issue as well.

Numerous Christians do not know how to glorify God in their eating and drinking. They do not eat and drink simply to keep their body fit for the Lord's use but indulge to satisfy their personal desires. We should understand that the body is for the Lord and not for ourselves; hence we should refrain from using it for our pleasure. Food ought not hinder our fellowship with God since it is to be taken purely to preserve the body in health.

The Apostle mentions the subject of immorality too. This is a sin which defiles the body: it directly contravenes the principle that "the body is for the Lord." Immorality here includes not just looseness outside the marriage relationship but overindulgence within marriage as well. The body is for the Lord, wholly for the Lord, not for oneself. Thus, license even in legitimate sexual intercourse is prohibited also.

The Apostle Paul's intent in this passage is to show us that any excess of the flesh must be thoroughly resisted. The body is for the Lord; the Lord alone can use it. The indulgence of any part solely for personal gratification is not pleasing to Him. Other than as an instrument of righteousness, the body is not to be used in any other way. It, like our entire being, cannot serve two masters. Even in such natural affairs as food and sex the body should be engaged exclusively to fill *needs*. While needs do require satisfaction, the body is nonetheless for the Lord and not for food and sex. Nowadays many Christians aspire to sanctification of their spirit and soul, not fully appreciating how greatly sanctification in these realms depends on sanctification of the body. They forget that unless all nerve responses, sensations, actions, conduct, works, food and speech which belong to the body are utterly for the Lord, they can never arrive at perfection.

"The body is for the Lord." This signifies that though the outer flesh belongs to the Lord it is entrusted to man for him to maintain for Him. How few are those who know and practice this truth! Many saints today are stricken with sickness, weakness and suffering; God is chastening them that they may present their bodies to Him a living sacrifice. They would be healed if they yielded them completely to God. God wants them to know that the body is for the Lord, not for themselves. If they continue to live according to their wishes they shall see the scourge of God remain upon them. All who are sick should take these words seriously to heart.

"And the Lord for the body." This is an incredibly wonderful statement! We usually think of the Lord as saving only our spirit and our soul, but here it is said that "the Lord (is) for the *body*." Christians look upon the Lord Jesus as having come to save their spirit and soul alone, that the body is useless, having no value in spiritual life and not graciously provided for in God's redemptive scheme. But it is plainly enunciated here that "the Lord is *for* the body." The Lord, affirms God, is equally for the earthen vessel which man lightly esteems.

"And God raised the Lord and will also raise us up by his power" (v.14). This is to explain the last clause of the preceding verse which is "the Lord for the body." The resurrection of the Lord is a *bodily* one: our future resurrection will therefore be *bodily* too. As God has already raised the body of the Lord Jesus so will He also raise ours from the dead. These two facts are equally certain. Hence this is how the Lord is for our body: He will raise us up by His power. It is yet future, nevertheless today we may foretaste the power of His resurrection.

"Do you not know that your body is a temple of the Holy Spirit within you, which you have from God?" (v.19). This is the second instance the Apostle Paul asks, "Do you not know?" The first occurred in verse 15 which spoke of "the body for the Lord." In this second instance he is referring to "the Lord for the body." Earlier Paul had expressed it in a general way as "*you* are God's temple" (3.16); now he says specifically that "*your body* is a temple of the Holy Spirit." It indicates that the habitation of the Holy Spirit is extended beyond the spirit to the body. We commit a signal error if we consider the body His primary dwelling place, for He dwells initially in our spirit where He holds fellowship with us. However, this does not preclude His life flowing from the spirit to make our body alive. We are deceived if we expect the Holy Spirit to descend primarily on our bodies; but we shall suffer loss, too, if we limit His dwelling place to our spirits.

"You are not your own; you were bought with a price. So glorify God in your body" (vv.19-20). You are members of Christ, you are a temple of the Holy Spirit, you are not your own. You were purchased by God with a price. Everything of yours belongs to Him, especially your body. The union of Christ with you and the seal of the Holy Spirit within you proves that your body particularly is God's. "So glorify God in your *body*." Brethren, God wishes us to honor Him there. He wants us to glorify Him both through the consecration of this "body for the Lord" of ours and also through the grace exhibited by the "Lord for the body" of His. Let us be sober and watchful lest we use our bodies for ourselves or permit them to fall into a condition as though the Lord were not for the body. Thus we shall glorify God and allow Him to demonstrate His power freely in delivering us from weakness, sickness and suffering as well as from self-interest, self-love and sin.

SICKNESS

This was to fulfill what was spoken by the prophet Isaiah, "He took our infirmities and bore our diseases."

Matthew 8.17

There are a few matters concerning sickness we would like to consider together before God:

1. THE RELATION BETWEEN SICKNESS AND SIN

Before the fall of mankind no infirmity of any kind existed; sickness arose only after man had sinned. One can say generally that both sickness and death resulted from sin; for by one man's trespass sin and death came into the world (Romans 5.12). Sickness spread to all men just as did death. Though not all sin in the same way as Adam did, yet because of his transgression, all die. Where there is sin there is also death. In between these two is that which we usually call sickness. This, then, is the factor common to all disease. However, there is actually more than one cause to account for sickness coming upon people. Some sicknesses spring from sin, while others do not. So far as *mankind* is concerned, sickness does come from sin; but in relation to the *individual* it may or may not be the case. We need to distinguish between these two applications of sickness. Now it is entirely true that were there no sin there could neither be death *nor* sickness; for if there were no death in the world, how could there ever be sickness? Death arises through sin, and sickness through the inception of death. Even so, this cannot be specifically and indiscriminately applied to every individual, because while many do fall ill through sin there are others who become ill for reasons other than sin. In this matter of the relationship of sin to sickness we must therefore make a careful distinction between the application of this relationship to mankind as a whole and its application to individual men.

The Scriptures have served sufficient notice that many (but not all) are ill because of sin. Hence the first action we must take when sick is to examine ourselves to determine whether or not we have sinned against God. By searching, many find that their illness is in fact due to sin: on a particular occasion they had rebelled against God or had disobeyed His Word. They had gone astray. Just as soon as that particular sin is found out and confessed, however, the sickness will be over. Countless brothers and sisters in the Lord have encountered such experiences. Shortly after the cause is discovered before God the illness is gone. This is a phenomenon beyond the explanation of medical science.

We unreservedly believe that there are natural explanations for sickness; this has been proven scientifically. We confess nonetheless that many illnesses among God's children are the consequences of sinning against God such as in the case cited in 1 Corinthians 11. It is consequently essential to ask for forgiveness first, then for healing afterwards. We frequently can detect, soon after we have been struck down with sickness, where we have transgressed against the Lord or how we have been disobedient to His Word. When the sin is confessed and the problem resolved, the sickness fades away. This is truly a most marvelous event. Thus the initial point we need to know is the relation between sin and sickness. Generally sickness results from sin; and individually, too, it may result from sin.

2. THE LORD'S WORK AND SICKNESS

"Surely he has borne our griefs and carried our sorrows; yet we esteemed him stricken, smitten by God, and afflicted. But he was wounded for our transgressions, he was bruised for our iniquities" (Isaiah 53.4-5). Of all the Old Testament writings this 53rd chapter of Isaiah is quoted most often in the New Testament. It alludes to the Lord Jesus Christ, especially to

Him as our Savior. Verse 4 affirms that "he has borne our griefs and carried our sorrows" whereas Matthew 8.17 declares that "this was to fulfil what was spoken by the prophet Isaiah, 'He took our infirmities and bore our diseases'." The Holy Spirit indicates here that the Lord Jesus came to the world to take our infirmities and bear our diseases. Prior to His crucifixion He had already taken our infirmities and borne our diseases; which is to say that during His earthly ministry the Lord Jesus made healing His burden and task. He not only preached, He also healed. He preached the glad tidings on the one hand, but on the other hand strengthened the weak, restored the withered hand, cleansed the leper and raised the palsied. While on earth the Lord Jesus devoted Himself to the performance of miracles as well as to the ministry of the Word. He went about doing good, He healed the sick, and cast out demons. The purpose of His work was to overthrow sickness, the result of sin. He came to deal with death and sickness as well as with sin.

There is a basic dissimilarity, however, between God's treatment of our iniquity and His treatment of our disease. Why this difference? Our Lord Jesus bore our sins in His body on the cross. Does any sin remain unforgiven? Absolutely none, for the work of God is so complete that sin is entirely destroyed. But in taking our infirmities and bearing our diseases while He lived on earth, the Lord Jesus did not eradicate all diseases and all infirmities. For note that Paul never says "when I sin, then am I sanctified," but he does declare that "when I am weak, then I am strong" (2 Corinthians 12.10). Hence sin is thoroughly and unlimitedly dealt with whereas sickness is only limitedly treated.

Nonetheless, we contend that since the Lord Jesus has actually borne our diseases there should not be so much sickness as there is among the children of God. While Jesus was on earth he unmistakably devoted Himself to the healing of the sick. He included healing in His work. Isaiah 53.4 is fulfilled in Matthew 8, not in Matthew 27. It is realized *before* Calvary. Had it been realized on the cross, healing would be unbounded. But no, the Lord Jesus bore our diseases prior to crucifixion, with the result that this aspect of His work is not as unlimited as was His bearing of our sins.

3. THE BELIEVER'S ATTITUDE TOWARDS SICKNESS

Every time the believer falls ill the first thing he should do is to inquire after its cause before the Lord. He should not be overanxious in seeking healing. Paul sets a good example in showing us how he was most clear about his weakness. We must examine whether we have disobeyed the Lord, have sinned anywhere, owe anybody a debt, have violated some natural law, or have neglected some special duty. We ought to know that frequently our violation of natural law can constitute a sin against God, for God sets up these natural laws by which to govern the universe. Many are afraid to die; upon becoming sick they hurriedly seek out physicians, for they are anxious to be cured. Such ought not to be the Christian's attitude. He should first attempt to isolate the cause for his malady. Alas, how many brothers and sisters do not possess any patience. The moment they fall sick they search for a remedy. Are you so afraid to lose your precious life that through prayer you lay hold of God for healing yet simultaneously lay hold of a physician for drugs and an injection? This reveals how full of self you are. But then how could you be less full of self in sickness if you are filled with self during ordinary days? Those who are ordinarily full of self will be those who anxiously seek for healing just as soon as they get sick.

Learn to accept whatever lesson sickness may bring to you. For if you have dealings with God many of your problems will be resolved quickly. You will find out that often your illness is due to some sin or fault of yours. Upon confessing your sin and asking for forgiveness, you may expect healing from God.

Or, should you have walked further with the Lord, you may discern that involved in this is the enemy's attack. Or the matter of God's discipline may be associated with your unhealthy state. God chastises with sickness so as to render you holier, softer or more yielding. As you deal with these problems before God you will be enabled to see the exact reason for your infirmity. Sometimes God may allow you to receive a little natural or medical help, but sometimes He may heal you instantaneously without such assistance.

4. THE WAY TO SEEK HEALING

How should men seek healing before God? Three sentences in the Gospel of Mark are worth learning. I find them especially helpful, at least they are very effective for me. The first touches upon the power of the Lord; the second, the will of the Lord; and the third, the act of the Lord.

a) The Power of the Lord: "God can." "And Jesus asked his father, 'How long has he had this?' And he said, 'From childhood. And it has often cast him into the fire and into the water, to destroy him; but *if you can* do anything, have pity on us and help us.' And Jesus said to him, '*If you can!* All things are possible to him who believes'" (9.21-23). The Lord Jesus merely repeated the three words which the child's father had uttered. The father cried, "If you can, help us." The Lord responded, "If you can! Why, all things are possible to him who believes." The problem here is not "if you can" but rather "if you believe."

Is it not true that the first problem which arises with sickness is a doubt about God's power? Under a microscope the power of bacteria seems to be greater than the power of God. Very rarely does the Lord cut off others in the middle of their speaking, but here he appears as though He were angry. (May the Lord forgive me for phrasing it this way!) When He heard the child's father say "If you can, have pity on us and help us," He sharply reacted with "Why say if you can? All things are possible to him who believes. In sickness, the question is not whether I can or cannot but whether you *believe* or not."

b) The Will of the Lord: "God will." Yes, He indeed can, but how do I know if He wills? I do not know His will; perhaps He does not want to heal me. This is another story in Mark again. "And a leper came to him beseeching him, and kneeling said to him, "If you will, you can make me clean. Moved with pity, he stretched out his hand and touched him, and said to him, "I will; be clean"" (1.40-41).

c) The Act of the Lord: "God has." One more thing must God do. "Verily I say unto you, Whosoever shall say unto this mountain, Be thou taken up and cast into the sea; and shall not doubt in his heart, but shall believe that what he saith cometh to pass; he shall have it. Therefore I say unto you, all things whatsoever ye pray and ask for, believe that ye receive (Gk. *received*) them, and ye shall have them" (11. 23-24 ASV). What is faith? Faith believes God can, God will, and God has done it. If you believe you have received it, you shall have it. Should God give you His word, you can thank Him by saying, "God has healed me; He has already done; it!" Many believers merely *expect* to be healed. Expectation regards things in the future, but faith deals with the past. If we really believe, we shall not wait for twenty or a hundred years, but shall rise up immediately and say, "Thank God He has healed me. Thank God, I have received it. Thank God, I am clean! Thank God, I am well." A perfect faith can therefore proclaim God can, God will and God has done it.

LESSON FORTY-ONE

GOD AS THE LIFE OF THE BODY

I came that they may have life, and have it abundantly.

John 10.10

No more need we look upon our outer shell as a miserable prison, for we can see in it the life of God being expressed. We now can experience in a deeper way that word which declares that "it is no longer I who live but Christ who lives in me." Christ has presently become the source of life to us. He lives in us today as He once lived in the flesh. We can thus apprehend more fully the implication of His pronouncement: "I came that they may have life, and have it abundantly" (John 10.10). This more abundant life suffices additionally for every requirement of our body. Paul exhorts Timothy to "take hold of the eternal life" (1 Timothy 6. 12); surely Timothy is not here in need of eternal life that he may be saved. Is not this life that which Paul subsequently describes in the same chapter as "the life which is life indeed" (v.19)? Is he not urging Timothy to experience eternal life today in overcoming every phenomenon of death?

We would hasten to inform our readers that we have not lost sight of the fact that our body is indeed a mortal one; even so, we who are the Lord's can verily possess the power of that life which swallows up death. In our body are two forces in action: death and life: on the one side is consumption which brings us nigh to death; on the other side is replenishment through food and rest and these support life. Now extravagant consumption weakens the body because the force of death is too powerful; but by the same token excessive supply reveals signs of congestion because the force of life is too strong. The best policy is to maintain these two forces of life and death in balance. Beyond this, we should understand that the weariness which believers often experience in their body is in many respects distinct from that of ordinary people. Their consumption is more than physical. Because they walk with the Lord, bear the burdens of others, sympathize with the brethren, work for God, intercede before Him, battle the powers of darkness, and pommel their body to subdue it, food and rest alone are insufficient to replenish the loss of strength in their physical frame. This explains in a measure why many believers, who before the call to service were healthy, find themselves physically feeble not long afterwards. Our bodily strength cannot cope with the demands of spiritual life, work, and war. Combat with sin, sinners, and the evil spirits saps our vitality. Solely natural resources are inadequate to supply our bodily needs. We must depend on the life of Christ, for this alone can sustain us. Should we rely on material food and nourishment and drugs we will be committing a serious blunder. Only the life of the Lord Jesus more than sufficiently meets all the physical requirements for our spiritual life, work, and war. He alone furnishes us the necessary vitality to grapple with sin and Satan. Once the believer has truly appreciated what spiritual warfare is and how to wrestle in the spirit with the enemy, he will begin to realize the preciousness of the Lord Jesus as life to his body.

The Lord's children today ought to know that He does care for their body. God is not only strength to our spirit He is equally so to our body. Even in the Old Testament time when grace was not manifested as much as it is today the saints experienced God as strength to their outer flesh. Can today's blessing be less than theirs? We should experience at least the same divine invigorating power as they did. If we are uninformed as to the riches of God, we perhaps may restrict them to what concerns our spirit. But those who have faith will not limit His life and power to the spirit by neglecting their application to the body.

We wish to underscore the fact that God's life is adequate not only to heal sickness but also to preserve us strong and healthy. God as our might enables us to overcome both illness and weakness. He does not heal so that we may live afterwards by our natural energy; *He* is to be energy to our body that we may live by Him and find power for all His service. When the Israelites left Egypt God promised them by saying, "If you will diligently hearken to the voice of the Lord your God, and do that which is right in his eyes, and give heed to his commandments and keep all his statutes, I will put none of the diseases upon you which I put upon the Egyptians; for I am the Lord, your healer" (Exodus 15.26). Later we find this promise wholly fulfilled as noted in Psalm 105: "there was not one feeble person among his tribes" (v.37 ASV). Let us hence understand that divine healing includes both God's curing our sicknesses and His withholding diseases from us that we may remain hardy. If we are totally yielded to God, resisting His will in nothing but believingly receiving His life as strength to our body, we shall yet prove the fact that Jehovah heals.

If we accept the Biblical teaching that our bodies are the members of Christ, we cannot but also acknowledge the teaching that the life of Christ flows through them. The life of Christ flows from the Head to the body, supplying energy and vitality to it. Since *our* bodies are members of *that* body, life naturally flows to them. This however needs to be appropriated by faith. The measure of faith by which we receive this life will determine the measure in which we actually experience it. From the Scriptures we have learned that the life of the Lord Jesus can be appropriated for the believer's body, but this requires faith. Doubtless Christians, when first exposed to such teachings, are struck with surprise. Yet we cannot dilute what the Word distinctly teaches. An examination of Paul's experience can assure us of the preciousness and reality of the teaching.

Paul, in referring to his physical condition, remarked about a thorn in his flesh. Three times he entreated the Lord concerning this, that it should be removed. But the Lord answered him, "My grace is sufficient for you, for my power is made perfect in weakness." And in response the Apostle said, "I will all the more gladly boast of my weaknesses, that the power of Christ may rest upon me . . . for when I am weak, then I am strong" (2 Corinthians 12.9-10). We need not inquire what that thorn was because the Bible does not divulge it. One point however is certain: the consequence of this thorn on the Apostle was that it weakened his body. The "weakness" here referred to is physical in nature. The same word is used in Matthew 8.17. The Corinthians were well acquainted with Paul's bodily frailty (2 Corinthians 10.10). Paul himself acknowledged that when he was with them the first time he was physically weak (1 Corinthians 2.3). His debility cannot be due to any lack of spiritual power, for both Corinthian letters reveal a powerful spiritual vigor in the Apostle.

From just these few passages we can gain insight into Paul's physical condition. He was very weak in body, but did he remain long therein? No, for he informs us that the power of Christ rested upon him and made him strong. We notice a "law of contrast" here. Neither the thorn nor the weakness which came from the thorn had left Paul; yet the power of Christ inundated his frail body and gave him strength to meet every need. The power of Christ was in contrast to the weakness of Paul. This power did not waft (take) the thorn away nor did it eliminate weakness, but it abided in Paul to handle whatever situation with which his weakened frame could not cope. It may be likened to a wick which though kindled with fire is not consumed because it is saturated with oil. The wick is as flimsy as ever, but the oil supplies everything the fire requires of it.

The Lord delights in flooding every nerve, capillary, and cell of our body with His might. He does not transform our enfeebled nature into a vigorous one, nor does he dispense a great deal of strength to be stored in us. He wants to be the life to our mortal flesh so that we may live *momentarily* by Him.

Perhaps some may think that to have the Lord Jesus as life to our body means God miraculously grants us a large measure of bodily power that we may never again suffer or be sick. But this was evidently not the experience of the Apostle, for does he not definitely declare that "we who live are always delivered unto death for Jesus' sake, that the life also of Jesus may be manifested in our mortal flesh"? Paul's flesh was frequently weakened, but the strength of the Lord Jesus continuously flowed into him. He lived momentarily by the life of the Lord. To accept Him as life for our body requires *constant trust*. In ourselves we cannot meet any situation at any time; but by trusting continually in the Lord we receive moment by moment all the necessary strength.

LESSON FORTY-TWO

OVERCOMING DEATH

I am the resurrection and the life; he who believes in me, though he die, yet shall he live, and whosoever lives and believes in me shall never die.

John 11.25-26

The experience of overcoming death is not unusual among saints. By the blood of the lamb the Israelites were protected from the hand of the death angel who slew the first-born of Egypt. In the name of the Lord, David was saved from the paws of the lion and the bear and also from the hand of Goliath. By casting some meal into the pot Elisha drove death out of it (2 Kings 4.38-41). Shadrach, Meshech and Abednego suffered no harm in the fiery furnace (Daniel 3.16-27). Daniel witnessed God shutting the mouths of the lions when he was thrown into their den. Paul shook off a deadly viper into the fire and experienced no harm (Acts 28.3-5). Enoch and Elijah both were raptured to heaven without tasting death—perfect examples of death being overcome.

It is God's aim to bring His children through the experience of overcoming death now. To triumph over sin, self, the world, and Satan is necessary; but victory is not complete without a corresponding triumph over death. If we wish to enjoy a complete victory we must destroy this *last* enemy (1 Corinthians 15.26). We will leave one foe unconquered if we fail to experience the triumph over death.

There is death in nature, death in us, and death from Satan. The earth lies under a curse; it is therefore ruled by that curse. If we desire to live victoriously on this earth, we will have to overcome the death which is in the world. Death is in our body. On the day we are born it begins to work in us; for which of us from that day onward does not commence traveling towards the tomb? Do not view death merely as a "crisis"; it is pre-eminently a progressive matter. It is already in us and is gradually and relentlessly devouring us. Our release from this earthly tent is but the crisic consummation of the protracted working of death. It can strike at our spirit, depriving it of life and power; it can strike at our soul, crippling its feeling, thought and will; or it can strike at our body, rendering it weak and sick.

In reading Romans 5 we find that "death reigned" (v.17). Death not only exists, it also reigns. It reigns in the spirit, in the soul, in the body. Although our body is still alive, death already is reigning in it. Its influence has not yet reached its zenith, but it is reigning nonetheless and pushing its frontiers so as to engulf the whole body. Various symptoms which we discover in our body demonstrate how much its power is upon us. And these lead people to that ultimate demise—physical death.

While there is the reign of death, there is also the reign of life (Romans 5.17). The Apostle Paul assures us that all who receive the abundance of grace and the free gift of righteousness "reign in life," a force which far exceeds the operative power of death. But Christians today have been so occupied with the problem of sin that the problem of death has virtually been forgotten. Important as the overcoming of sin is, the overcoming of death—a related problem—should not be neglected. We know Romans Chapters 5 to 8 deal very distinctly with the matter of overcoming sin, but it gives equal attention to the question of death: "the wages of sin is death" (6.23). Paul deals with the consequence of sin as well as with sin itself. He not only contrasts righteousness and trespasses but also compares life and death. Many Christians stress overcoming the various manifestations of sin in their character and daily life, yet they fail to emphasize how to overcome the result of sin, namely, death. The Apostle, however, is used by God in these few chapters to discuss not so much sin's manifestations in daily life as sin's consequence which is death.

We must see clearly the relationship between these two elements. Christ died to save us not only from our sins but from death as well. God is now calling us to subdue both these phenomena. As sinners we were dead in sins, for sin and death reigned over us; but the Lord Jesus in His death for us has swallowed up our sin and death. Death at first reigned in our body, but being identified with His death we have died to sin and been made alive to God (6.11). Because of our union with Christ "death no longer has dominion over him (us)" nor can it bind us anymore (6.9,11). The salvation of Christ replaces sin with righteousness and death with life. Since the main objective of the Apostle in this portion of Scripture is to deal with sin and death, our acceptance cannot be complete if we absorb only half the theme. Paul describes the full salvation of the Lord Jesus in these terms: "the law of the Spirit of life in Christ Jesus has set me free from the law of sin and death" (8.2). Granted we have a great amount of experience in overcoming sin, yet how much have we experienced the overcoming of death?

To overcome death believers must alter their attitude from one of submission to one of resistance towards it. Unless we cast off our *passive* approach we will not be able to overthrow death but will be mocked by it instead and finally come to an untimely end. Numerous saints today misapprehend passivity for faith. They reason that they have committed everything to God. If they ought not to die, He verily shall save them from it: if they ought to die, then He doubtless shall allow them to die: let the will of God be done. Such a saying *sounds* right, but is this faith? Not at all. It is simply a lazy passivity. When we *do not know* God's will, it is fitting for us to pray: "not my will, but thine, be done" (Luke 22.42). This does not mean we need not pray *specifically*, letting our requests be made known to God. We should not submit passively to death, for God instructs us to work together actively with His will. Except we *definitely know* God wants us to die, we must not passively permit death to oppress us. Rather, we must actively cooperate with God's will to resist it.

Three different ways are open for Christians to overcome death: (1) by trusting we will not die until our work is finished; (2) by having no fear of death even should it come because we know its sting has been removed; and (3) by believing we will be delivered completely from death since we shall be raptured at the Lord's return. Let us ponder these one by one.

DEATH AFTER OUR WORK IS FINISHED

Unless a Christian plainly knows his work is finished and he no longer is required by the Lord to remain, he should by all means resist death. If the symptoms of death have been seen already in his body before his work is done, he positively should resist it and its symptoms. He should believe that the Lord will undertake in what he has resisted, for He has work for him yet to do. Hence before our appointed task is discharged we can trust in the Lord restfully even in the face of dangerous physical signs. In cooperating with the Lord and resisting death we will soon see Him work towards the swallowing up of it by His life.

Notice how the Lord Jesus resisted the jaws of death. When people tried to push Him down a cliff He passed through the midst of them and went His way (Luke 4.29-30). On one occasion "Jesus went about in Galilee; (but) he would not go about in Judea, because the Jews sought to kill him" (John 7.1). On another occasion the Jews "took up stones to throw at him; but Jesus hid himself, and went out of the temple" (John 8.59). Why did He thrice resist mortality? Because His time had not yet come. He knew there was an appointed hour for the Messiah to be cut off; He could not die in advance of

God's appointed moment nor could He die at any other place than at Golgotha. We too must not die before our time.

Overcoming death does not necessarily mean no grave, for God may wish some to overcome it through resurrection just as our Lord Jesus did. In passing through death believers, like their Lord, need have *no fear of it*. If we seek to overcome the jaws of death because we are afraid or unwilling to die, we already are defeated. It may be that the Lord will save us from death altogether by rapturing us alive to heaven; we nonetheless should not ask for His speedy return out of a fear of mortality. Such apprehensiveness shows we are defeated already by death. Let us come to see that even should we go to the grave we are merely walking from one room to another room. There is no justification for unbearable inward pain, fear and trembling.

We originally were "those who through fear of death were subject to lifelong bondage" (Hebrews 2.15). The Lord Jesus, however, has set us free and therefore we fear it no more. Its pain, darkness and loneliness cannot frighten us. An Apostle who had experienced victory over death testified that "to die is gain. . . . My desire is to depart and be with Christ, for that is *far better*" (Philippians 1.21,23). Not a wrinkle of fear could be detected there. The victory over death was actual and complete.

RAPTURED ALIVE

We know that at the return of the Lord Jesus many will be raptured alive. This is the last way of overcoming death. Both 1 Corinthians 15.51-52 and 1 Thessalonians 4.14-17 discuss this way. We realize there is no set date for the Lord's coming. He could have come at any time during the past twenty centuries. Hence believers always could cherish the hope of being raptured without passing through the grave. Since the coming of the Lord Jesus is currently much nearer than before our hope of being raptured alive is greater than that of our predecessors. We do not wish to say too much, but these few words we can safely affirm; namely, *should* the Lord Jesus come in our time, would we not want to be living so as to be raptured alive? If so, then we must overcome death, not letting ourselves die before our appointed hour so that we may be raptured alive. According to the prophecy of Scripture, some believers shall be raptured without going through death. To be thus raptured constitutes one more kind of victory over death. As long as we remain alive on earth we cannot deny we may be the ones to be so raptured. Should we not therefore be prepared to overcome death completely?

The Lord Jesus expressed this view at the death of Lazarus: "I am the resurrection and the life; he who believes in me, though he die, yet shall he live, and whoever lives and believes in me shall never die" (John 11.25-26). Here the Lord is not only the resurrection but also the life. However, most of us believe Him as the resurrection, yet forget that He also is the life. We readily admit He will raise us up after we die, but do we equally acknowledge that He, because He is our life, is able to keep us alive? The Lord Jesus explains to us His two kinds of work, yet we only believe in one. Believers throughout these twenty centuries shall have experienced the Lord's word that "he who believes in me, though he die, yet shall he live"; certain others shall enjoy in the future His other word that "whoever lives and believes in me shall *never die*." Thousands and thousands of believers already have departed in faith; but God says some shall never die—not some shall never be raised again, but, some shall *never die*. Consequently we have no reason to insist that we first must die and subsequently be resurrected. Since the coming of the Lord Jesus is nigh, why should we die beforehand and wait for resurrection? Why not expect the Lord to come and rapture us that we may be delivered totally from the power of death?

OTHER TITLES AVAILABLE FROM CHRISTIAN FELLOWSHIP PUBLISHERS

By Watchman Nee

Basic Lesson Series

Volume 1—A Living Sacrifice
Volume 2—The Good Confession
Volume 3—Assembling Together
Volume 4—Not I, But Christ
Volume 5—Do All to the Glory of God
Volume 6—Love One Another

CD ROM — The Complete Works of Watchman Nee

Aids to "Revelation"
Back to the Cross
A Balanced Christian Life
The Better Covenant
The Body of Christ: A Reality
The Character of God's Workman
Christ the Sum of All Spiritual Things
The Church and the Work
Come, Lord Jesus
The Communion of the Holy Spirit
The Finest of the Wheat— Volume 1
The Finest of the Wheat—Volume 2
From Faith to Faith
From Glory to Glory
Full of Grace and Truth—Volume 1
Full of Grace and Truth—Volume 2
Gleanings in the Fields of Boaz
The Glory of His Life
God's Plan and the Overcomers
God's Work
Gospel Dialogue
Grace for Grace
Interpreting Matthew
The King and the Kingdom of Heaven
The Latent Power of the Soul

Let Us Pray
The Life that Wins
The Lord My Portion
The Messenger of the Cross
The Ministry of God's Word
The Mystery of Creation
Powerful According to God
Practical Issues of This Life
The Prayer Ministry of the Church
The Release of the Spirit
Revive Thy Work
The Salvation of the Soul
The Spirit of Judgment
The Spirit of the Gospel
The Spirit of Wisdom and Revelation
Spiritual Authority
Spiritual Knowledge
The Spiritual Man
Spiritual Reality or Obsession
Take Heed
The Testimony of God
Whom Shall I Send?
The Word of the Cross
Worship God
Ye Search the Scriptures

By Stephen Kaung

Discipled to Christ
The Songs of Degrees—*Seeing the Lord's End in Job*
The Splendor of His Ways—*Meditations on Fifteen Psalms*

6 - 26 - 2013

2 - 11 - 16
also just finished the
full Spiritual Man
before this

10-13-21. this last 5 pages
have released a great
weakness I have
been going through. I
am now stronger &
full of Jesus strength
to meet the day.
Wilma W.